Cemeteries of Southwest Virginia

Exploring Appalachian Burial Grounds

H. A. Hutson

America Through Time

Open book at the feet in Hutson Cemetery, private woodlands.

AMERICA THROUGH TIME®
An imprint of SUTTON PUBLISHING INC.
www.through-time.com

First published 2025

ISBN 978-1-63499-539-9

Typeset in 10pt on 13pt Sabon
Printed and bound in England

Introduction

The Cemeteries of Southwest Virginia are part of the Appalachian Region of the United States. The immigrants who settled here were fleeing political and religious upheaval and oppression, servitude, and law enforcement in the Americas. These roots created a culture of stubborn and independent people. This developed a culture apart from any other that would come about in the new world. Even today, that otherness is a prevalent sentiment.

Early cemeteries and graveyards of the area are tucked away in private cemeteries on farms or in forests that have grown up to conceal them. Some are graveyards that stand adjacent to the churches from which they sprung. Some are all that is left of places where a church once stood, but over time were reclaimed by the environment after being abandoned.

But inside the cemetery gates is a cultural story that warrants a closer look. The residents of these graves saw the birth of a new nation or fought to maintain the independence their forefathers died to achieve. Their descendants lived during the rise of the industrial revolution and others for the fall of the same. Throughout the centuries there have been patriots of every war. All of this is reflected in stone, and sometimes other materials, tucked away on the outskirts of our communities or lost in the backwoods of Appalachia.

Join us as we take a walk through the cemeteries of Southwest Virginia, exploring Appalachian burial grounds.

Cemeteries of Southwest Virginia

The cemeteries of Southwest Virginia may seem ordinary enough—rows upon rows of etched and shining marble or, in the more modern cemeteries, slabs embedded in the ground for convenience. Yet travel into the backwoods and down the country roads to historic towns and you will find burial grounds that encompass centuries of culture and heritage. The oldest remnants of Appalachia's evolution are mostly lost to time, weather-worn to nubs or completely deteriorated back into the earth.

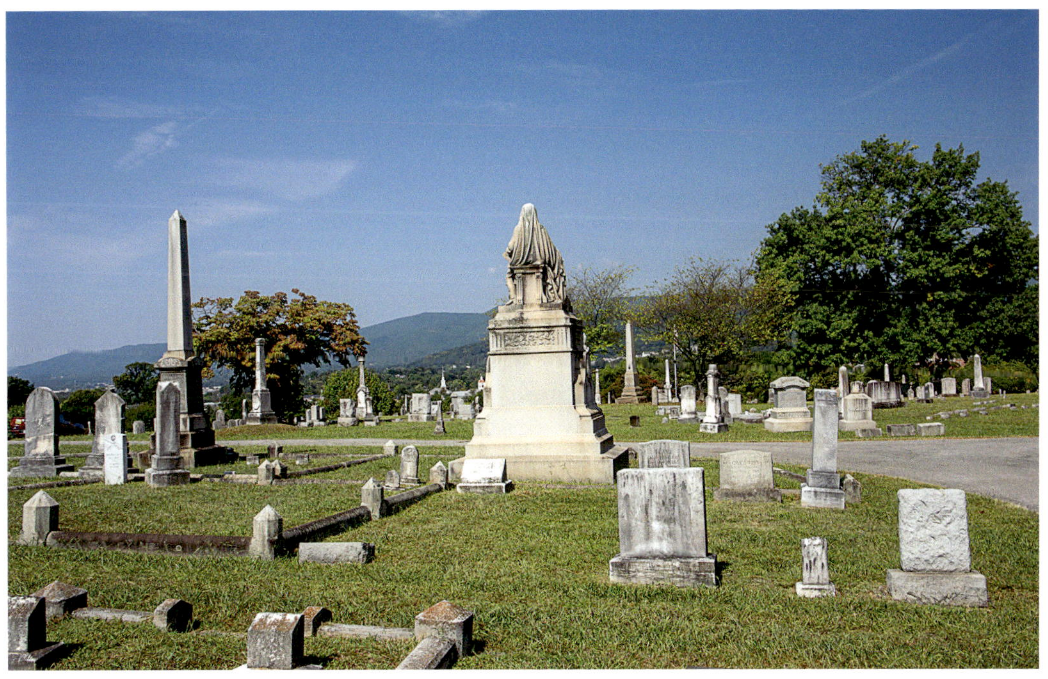

East Hill Historic cemetery, Salem, Virginia. The first burials here were during the Civil War in an abandoned Baptist churchyard. The cemetery was officially established in 1869.

The culture itself remained intact until very recently, and in some pockets of Southwest Virginia and throughout Appalachia, it remains untouched. Cemeteries with everything from timeworn grave markers to towering memorials to the Industrial Revolution, heartfelt loss, and multiple wars are tucked away in every corner. Everything from simple monuments to truly elaborate statements can be found all in one place.

Before this book gets underway, there are a few distinctions to be made. There is a difference between cemeteries and graveyards: cemeteries are very inclusive of an entire population, while graveyards are more restricted to the parishioners of that church. However, the further back in time you go, the more likely that the older churches were in and of themselves representative of that community.

A cemetery is a freestanding burial ground that is not adjacent to, and often is not associated with, any one religious organization or church. They are often built specifically for a community that may have a variety of belief systems, thereby avoiding conflict for families who may span several of these organizations. In some cases, the decedent may not have held a particular religious preference or had a request specifically not to be laid to rest in a religiously established way.

Graveyards are adjacent to a church structure, usually of a particular denomination. This is why it is not uncommon to find small graveyards and then freestanding cemeteries in close proximity to one another.

The symbolism on tombstones may also be affected in the same way. Sometimes a symbol can have more than one meaning because different cultures, religions, or even denominations within a religion have different ideas for that image. Where possible, this publication will note all possible interpretations.

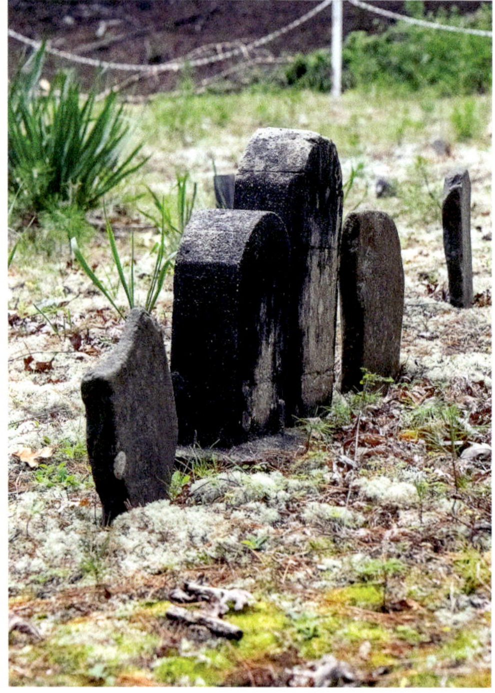

Stones worn to unknowns. Unnamed backwoods cemetery on Blacksburg Road, Virginia.

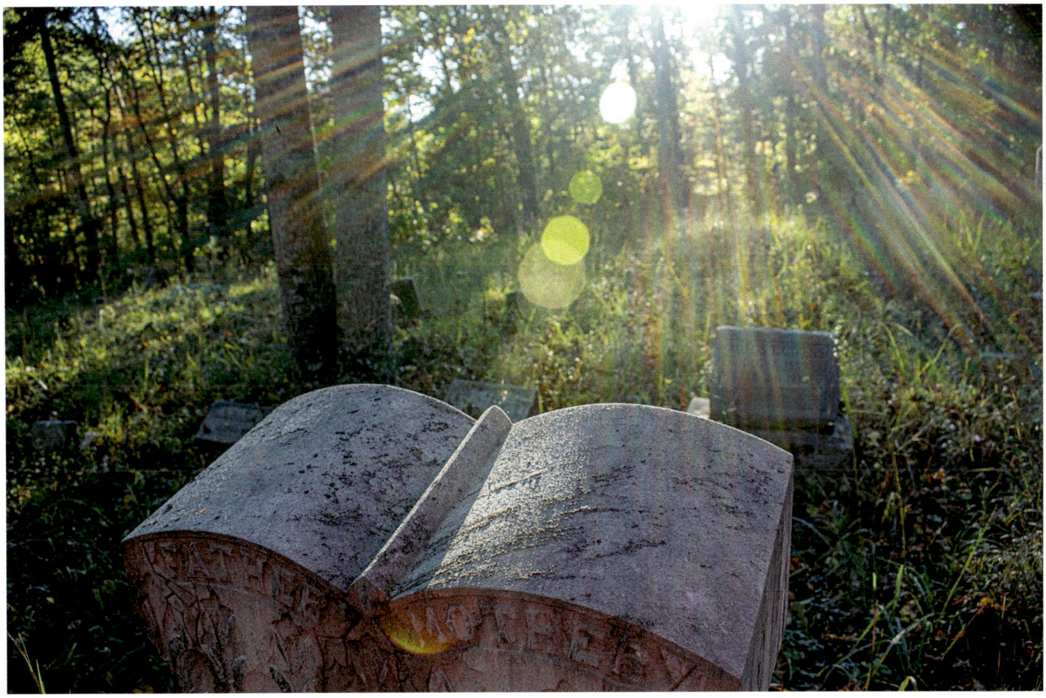

McCartney Cemetery, Craig County, Virginia. Backwoods cemetery on the edge of Jefferson National Forest.

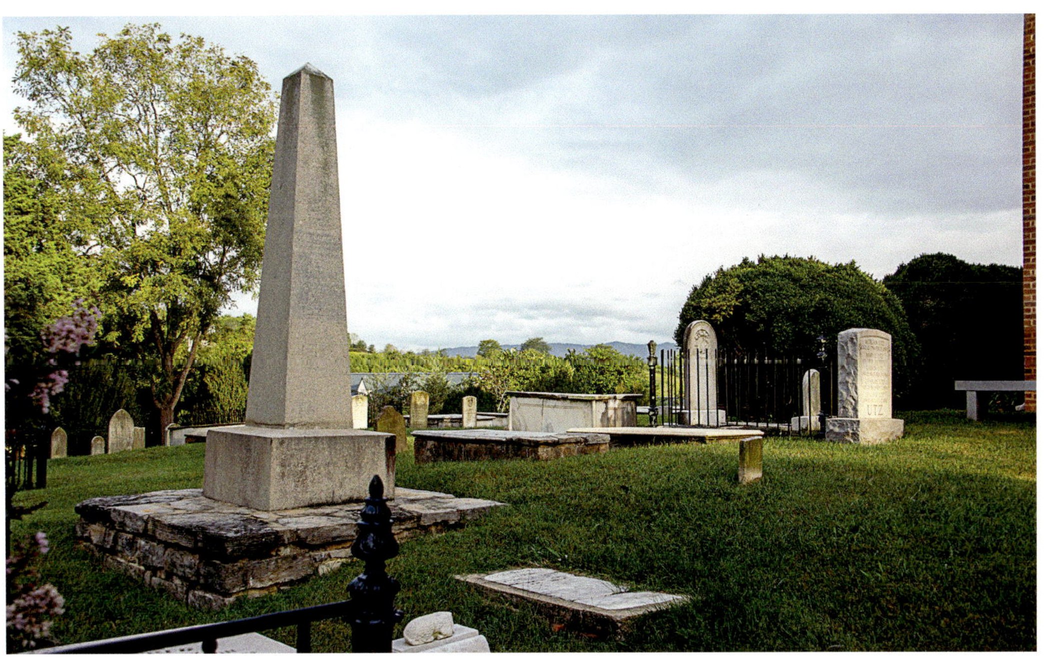

Fincastle Presbyterian Church Graveyard. Originally the Church of England, it became Presbyterian after the American Revolution.

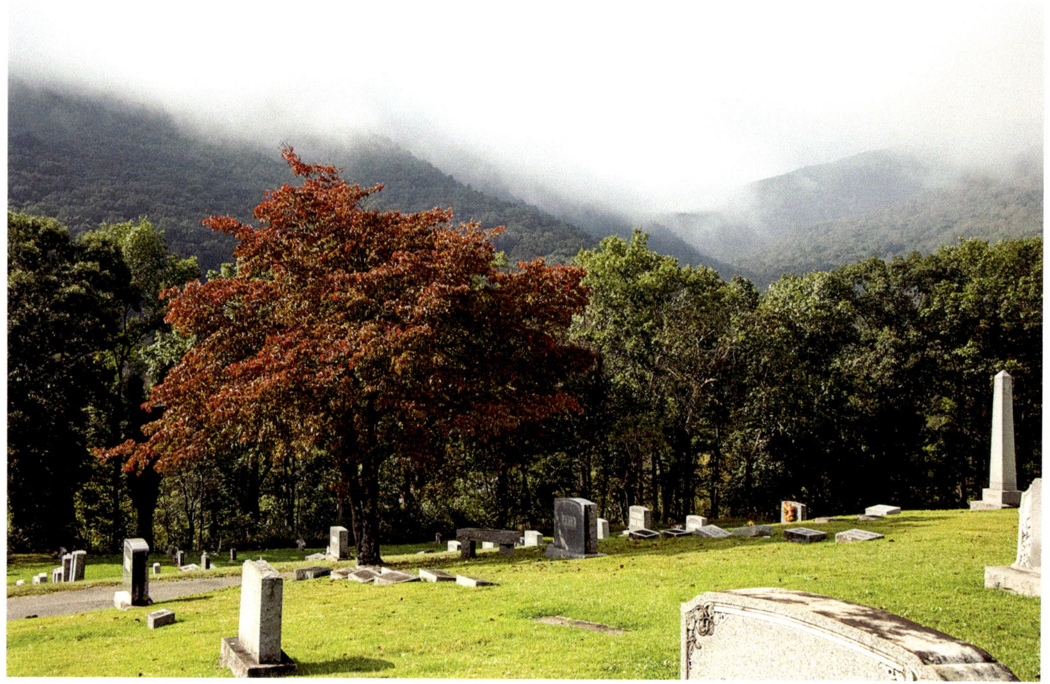

Mountain View Cemetery, Clifton Forge, Virginia. A typical view of the Appalachian region in Southwest Virginia. Rolling green mountains and mist on an early fall day.

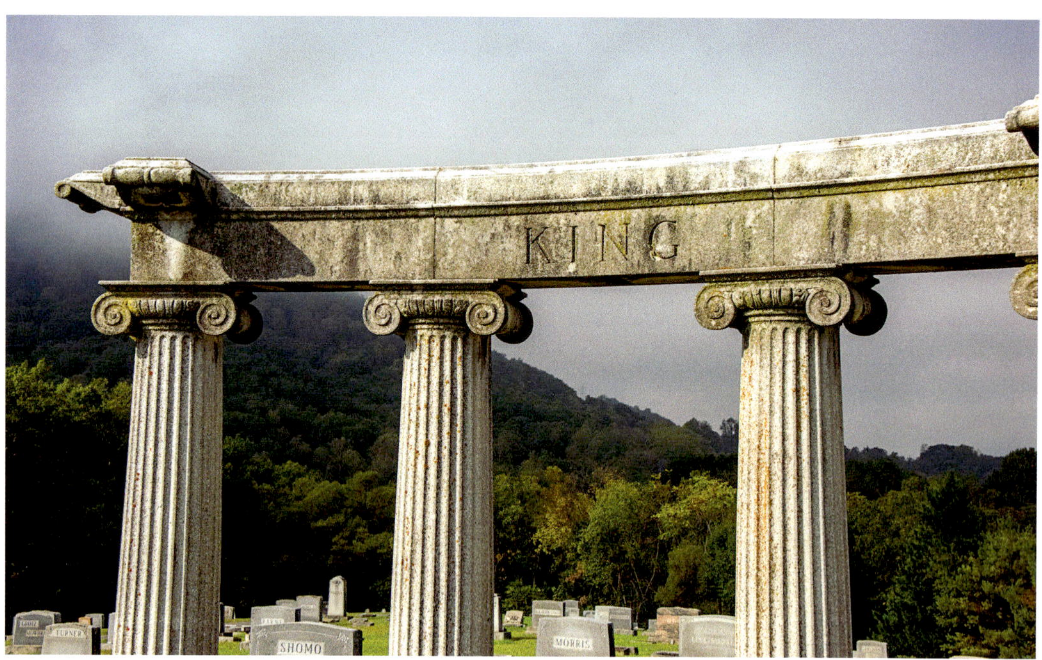

Mountain View Cemetery, Clifton Forge, Virginia. The King family plot.

Burial customs have varied widely on a regional level within the United States—more so in the past than the present. The Appalachian region, however, held on to its heritage and culture more fervently than other areas. Materials used to mark graves were what was at hand. Many of the stones in this region are soft enough to weather poorly, leaving only shadows of evidence they were here. The Appalachian range existed before bone developed. Its deepest layers reflect this in the lack of fossils that only appear in much more recent layers, geologically speaking. Deep in these mountains are caves that reach into pockets of the time before animals with bones emerged. This bears an eerie testament to a time to which only this mountain range bore witness. That is why this range is not as tall as the mountain ranges elsewhere. It has been worn by millennia of storms and temperature swings to stooped rolling mountains that reflect its age.

Perhaps that is why immigrants descended from the oldest bloodlines of Europe found Appalachia to be a siren's song. To the Scottish, it felt like home. The Scottish Highlands are related to the Appalachian Mountains because they were part of the same mountain range. Known as the Central Pangean Mountains, these two regions were connected before geological movements separated the continents. This certainly made it feel like home when, due to political pressure, many Scotts came to the Americas to start a new life.

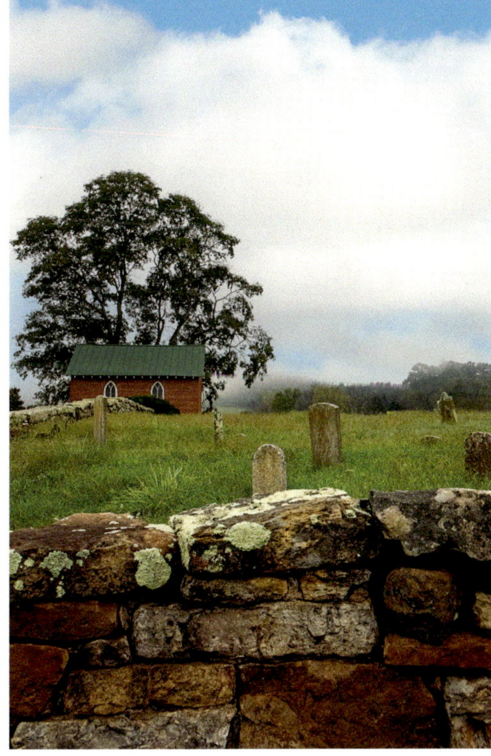

Locust Bottom Graveyard, which is now labeled a cemetery because the church is only a historic building and is not an active church. This historic cemetery houses Revolutionary War graves and is still an active cemetery for the local community.

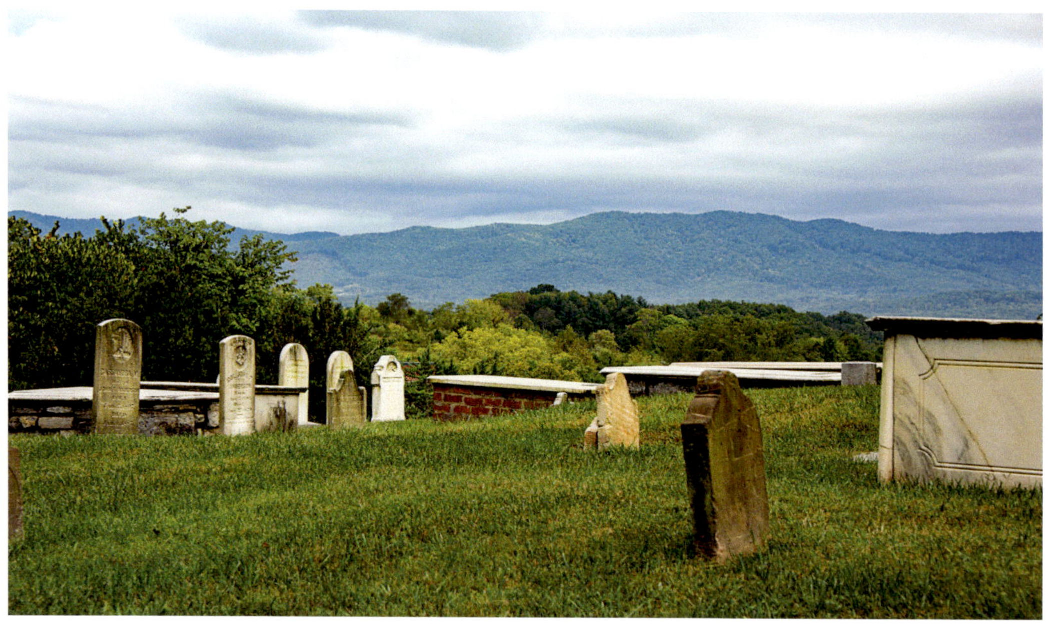

Fincastle Presbyterian Church, overlooking the Civil War-era section of the cemetery with the Blue Ridge Mountains in the background.

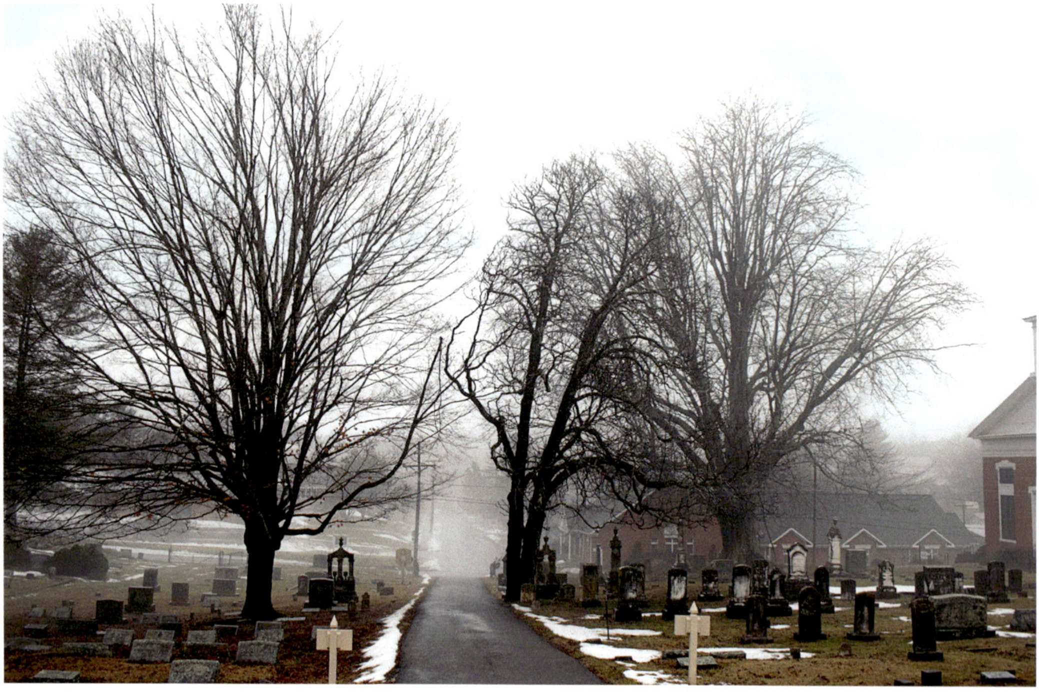

Godwin Graveyard, adjacent to United Methodist Church, Fincastle, Virginia, was founded around mid-1801 by James Godwin, originally as a family plot. It eventually became a community graveyard.

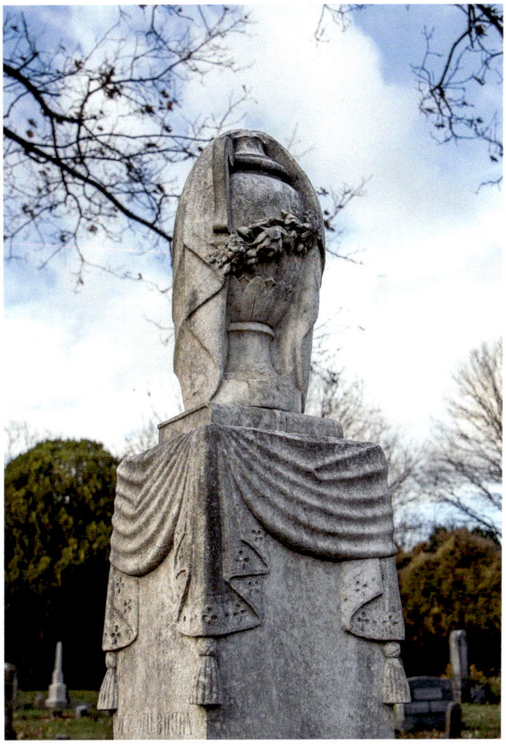

Symbolism in cemeteries can tell a story. This stone carries several symbols. The urn and tassels mean mourning and loss, the daisy represents gentleness and innocence, a rose only part open means a death in young adulthood, greenery conveys unspoken thoughts, mourning cloth is the separation of life and death.

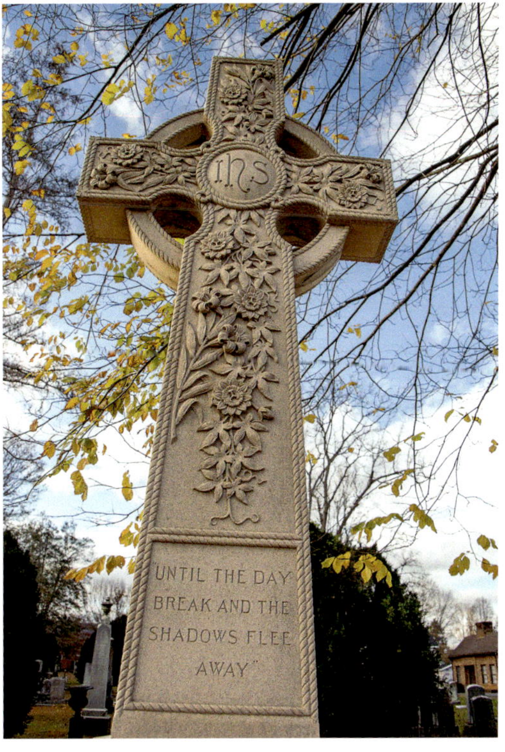

The cross combined with IHS stands for "Iesus Hominem Salvator," Latin for "Jesus Savior of Mankind." Easter lilies represent resurrection and innocence of the soul. Daffodils indicate grace, beauty, and deep regard. Greenery represents unspoken thoughts.

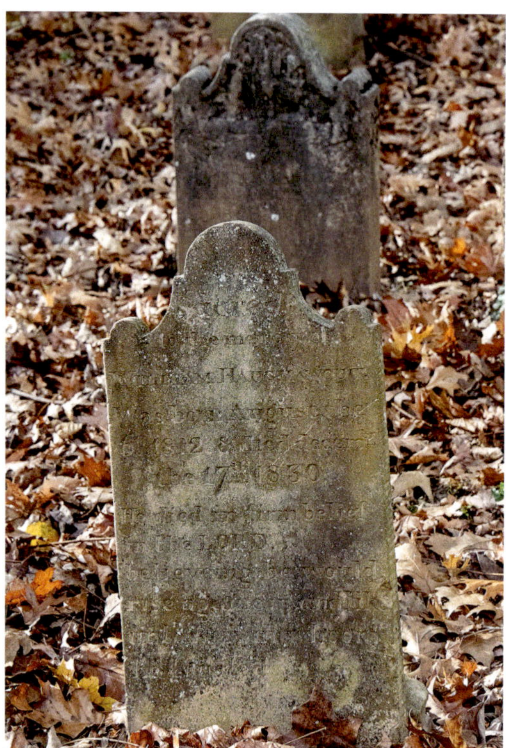

Left: The softer native stones of the region weather poorly, leaving them illegible. The identities are eventually lost to time and weather. Once they have passed from the living memories of those who knew them, they often become unrecognized graves known only to a dusty ledger that may not itself survive.

Below: A timeworn stone, barely legible, Fincastle Presbyterian graveyard.

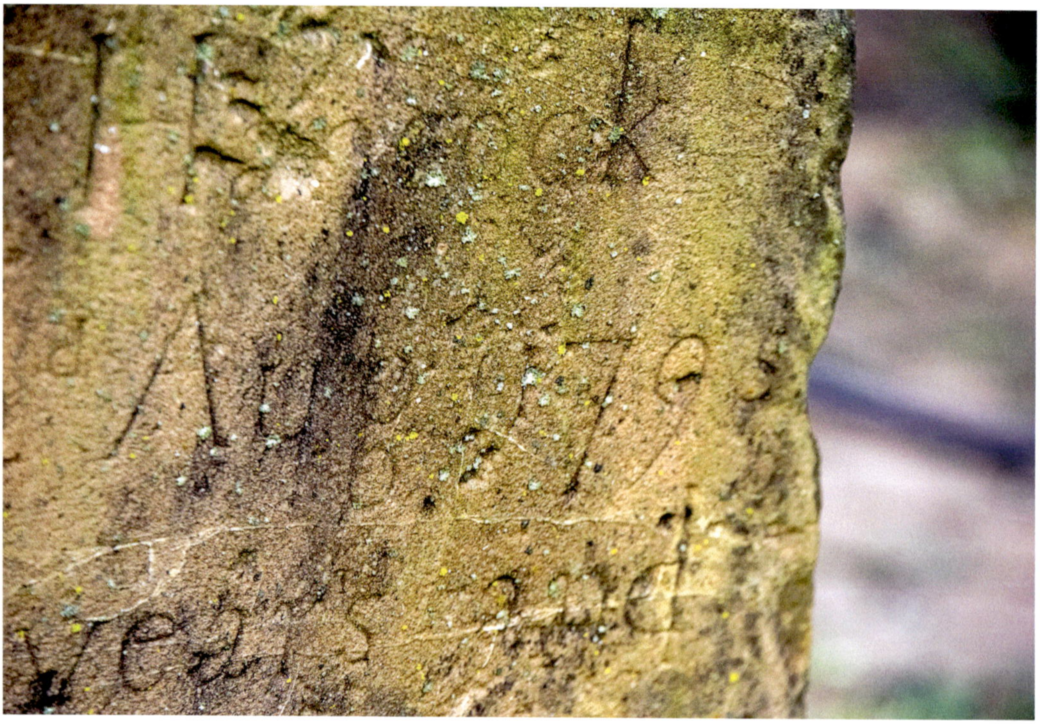

These mountainous regions were once a magnet for immigration and became a melting pot of hope for people who were coming here for a myriad of reasons. The first to arrive (but not for settlement) were the Spanish, exploring from modern-day Florida up through the mountain chain which reaches nearly to Canada. The Spanish found complex societies of Native Americans and introduced trade, building a business route with incoming Europeans. This would give rise to the traditions of Appalachia, including funerary rites and burial grounds.

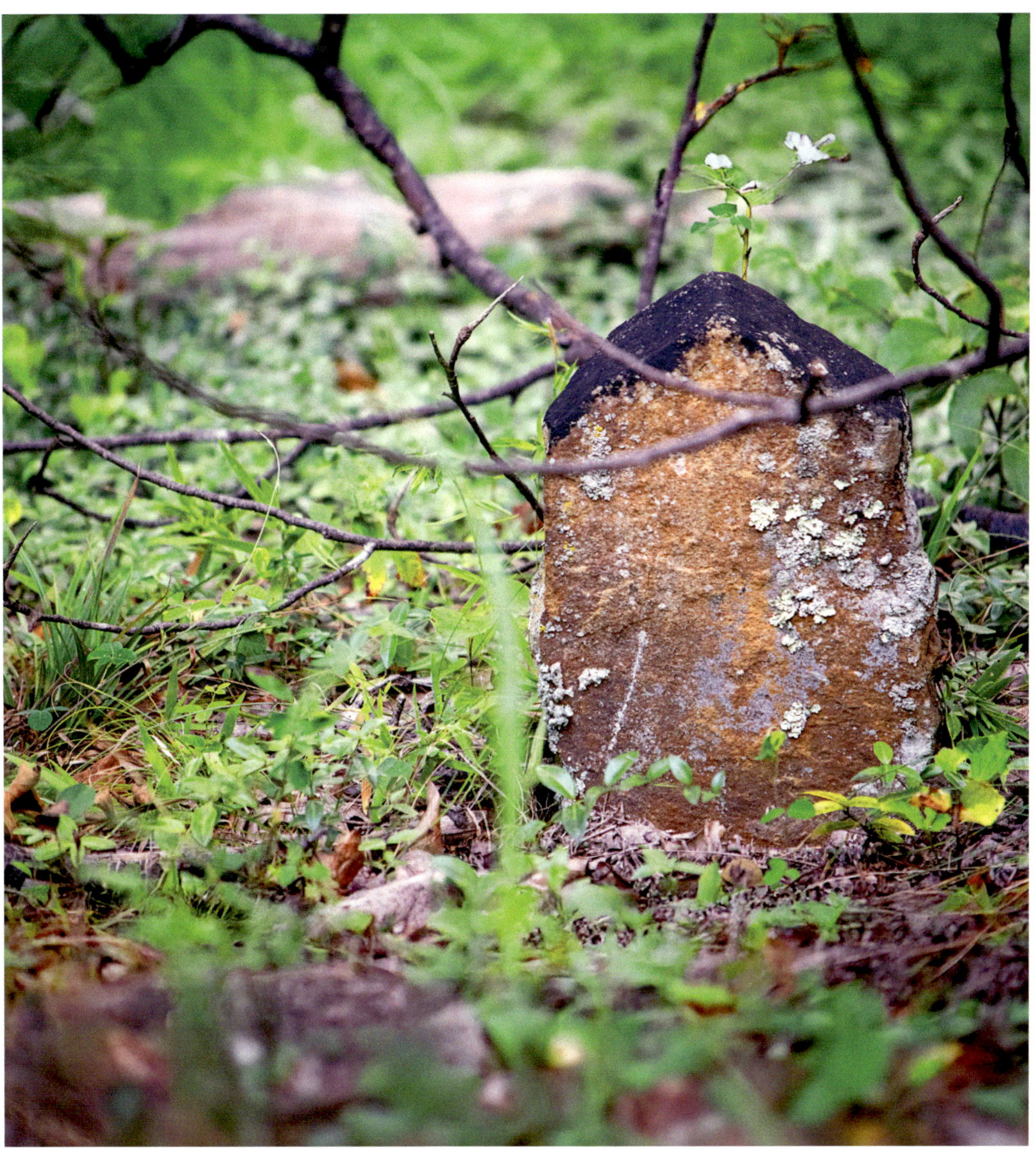

Soft mountain stone worn until it is barely recognizable as a tombstone in an unnamed cemetery in the Southwest Virginia woods, likely early 1700s.

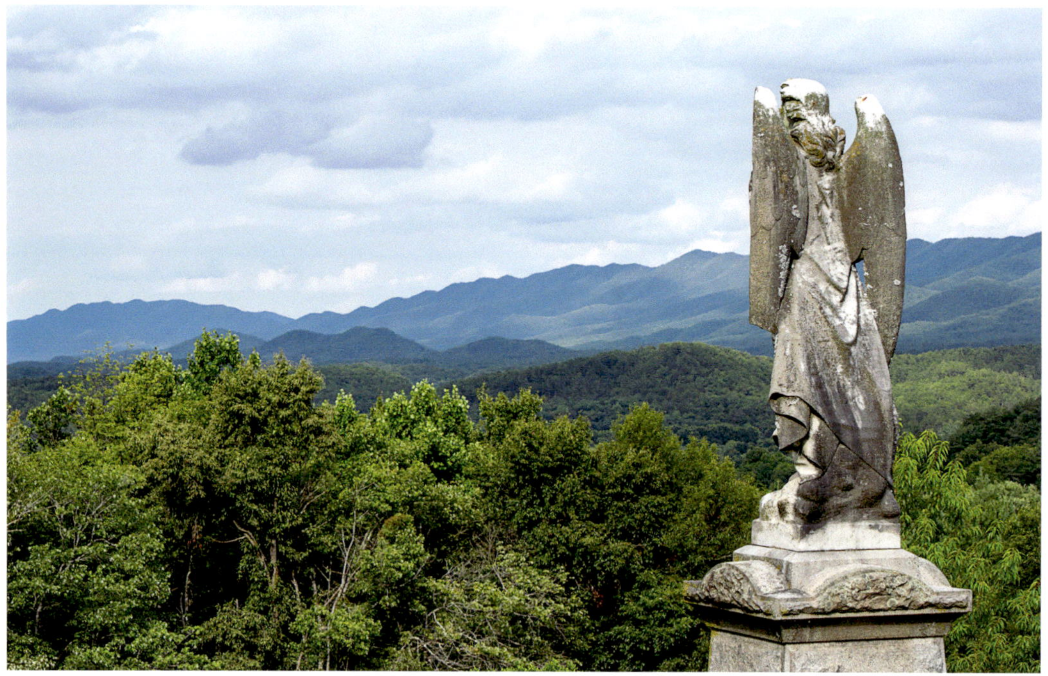

Angel monument overlooking West View Cemetery in New Castle, Virginia, with the Blue Ridge Mountains (part of the Appalachian region) in the background.

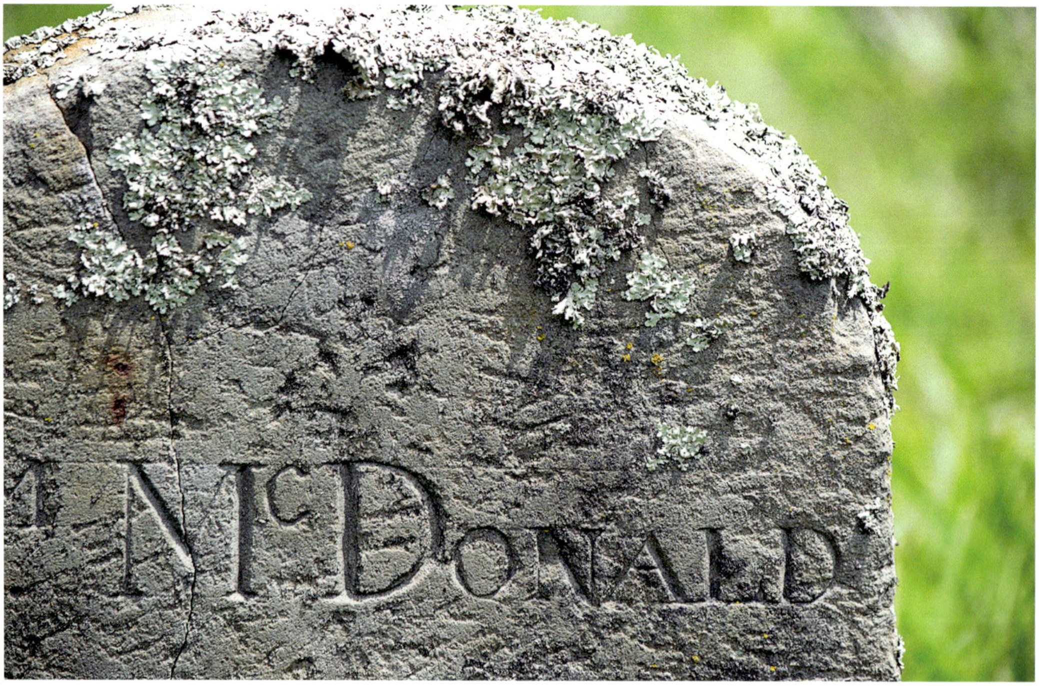

McDonald is a common Scottish name in our cemeteries. Mt Union Cemetery, Troutville, VA.

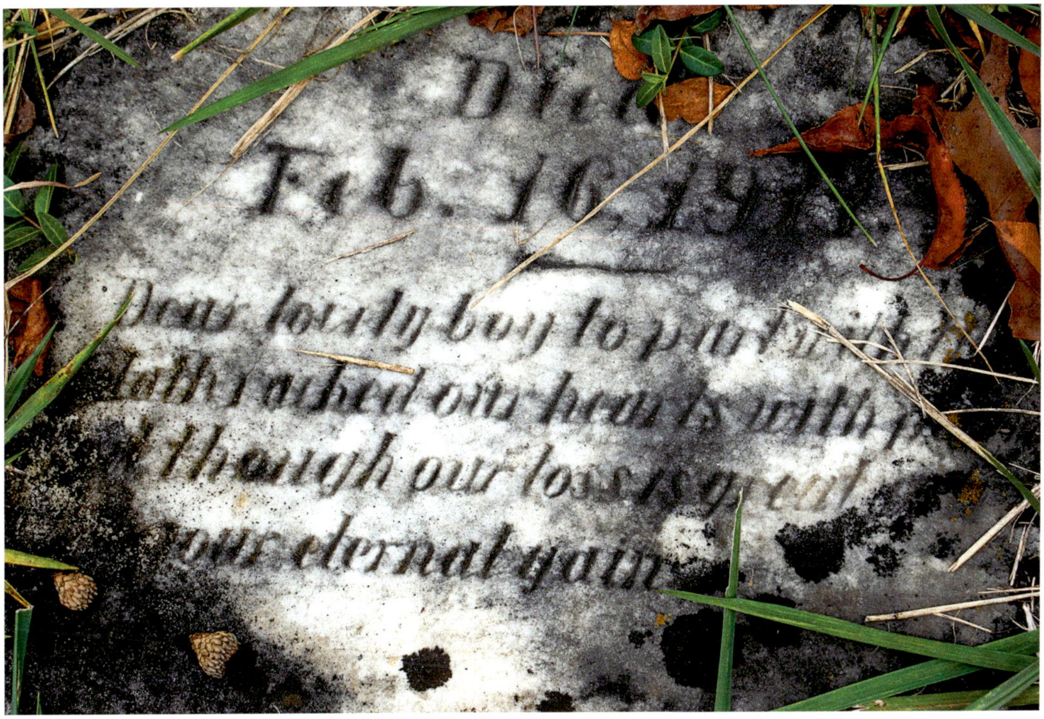

Above: Child's grave in a forgotten cemetery in the forest. "Dear lovely boy to part with thee hath razed our hearts with pain ... though our loss is great ... your eternal gain."

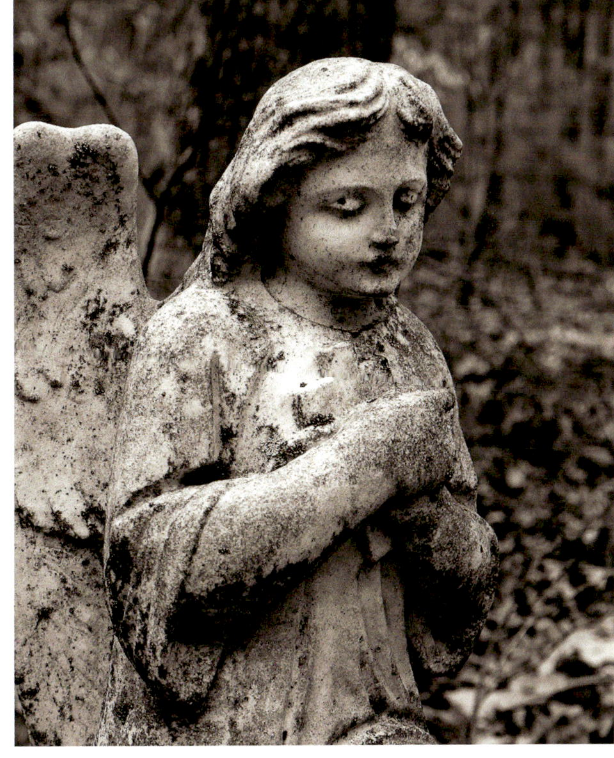

Right: Angel in Hutson Cemetery, private woodlands in Giles County, Virginia.

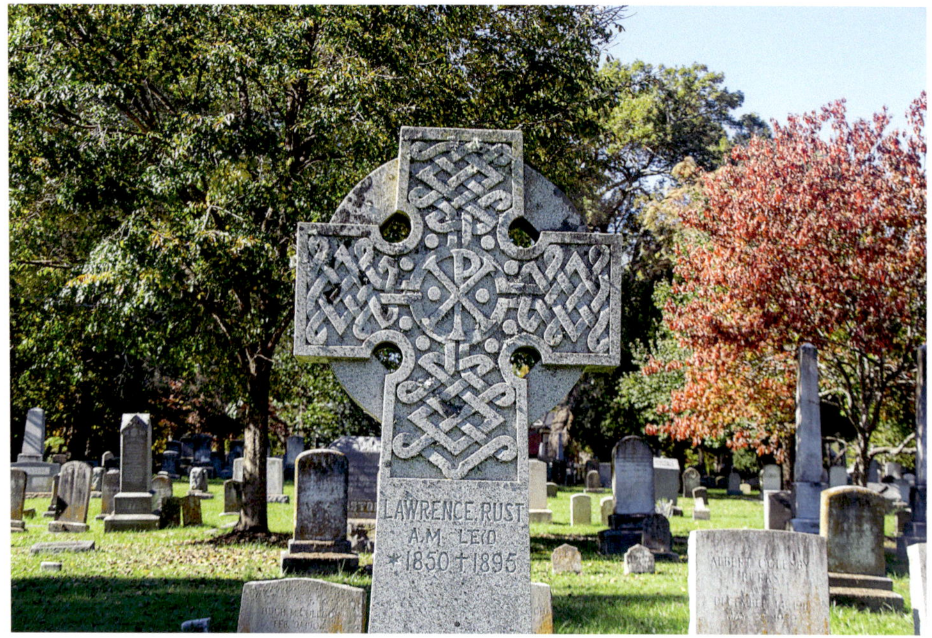

Celtic-style carved stone, Oak Grove Cemetery, Lexington, Virginia. Irish immigrants were very common in the region as many Irish and Scottish were drawn to the Appalachian Mountains.

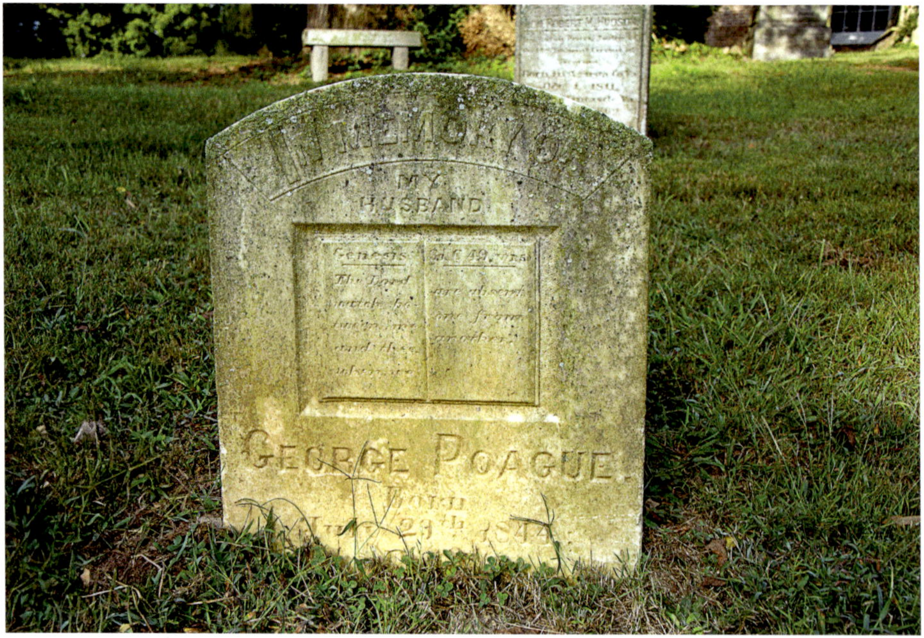

Scottish surnames are found throughout the older cemeteries. Fincastle Presbyterian graveyard.

In the early to mid-1700s, settlers began to arrive, mostly from the British Isles and Germany due to ongoing political turmoil. Lowland Scotland and what is modern-day Northern Ireland are of particular interest in regard to the region in question. They were fleeing oppression and constant military rule—which plays into many of the cultural developments. Their distrust of governments and monarchies that had persecuted them for hundreds of years caused a push into the backwoods where they could build self-sustaining lives. They brought with them an enslaved population. By 1860, 10 percent of the population was black—mostly enslaved. There are sparce remnants of those cemeteries remaining.

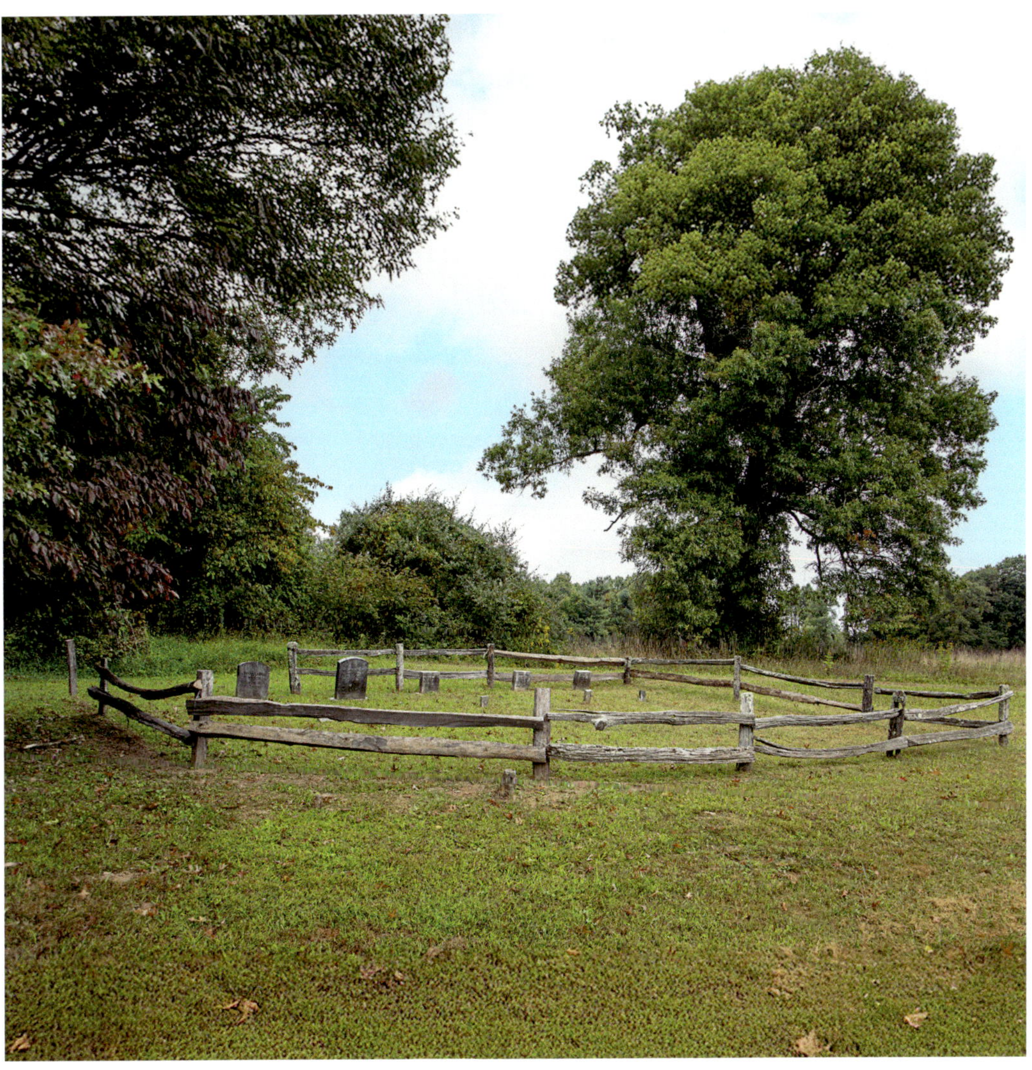

Wilson Cemetery on the Blue Ridge Parkway in Southwest Virginia is a prime example of rural cemeteries in the mountains. Often churches were too far to go, and families liked to have their loved ones close.

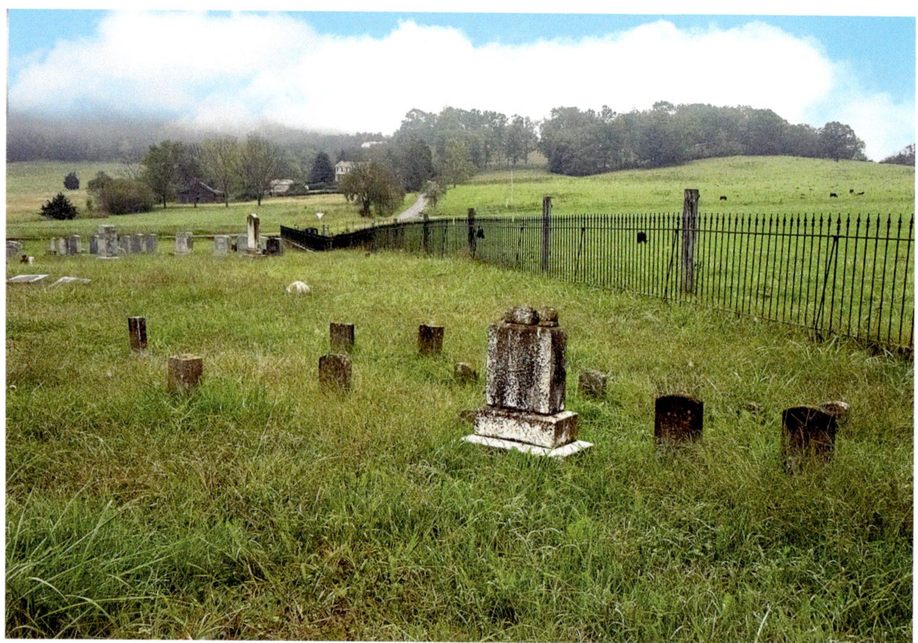

Locust Bottom Cemetery, Botetourt County backroads, was a community graveyard adjacent to the church. The church is a historic site now, maintained by the community.

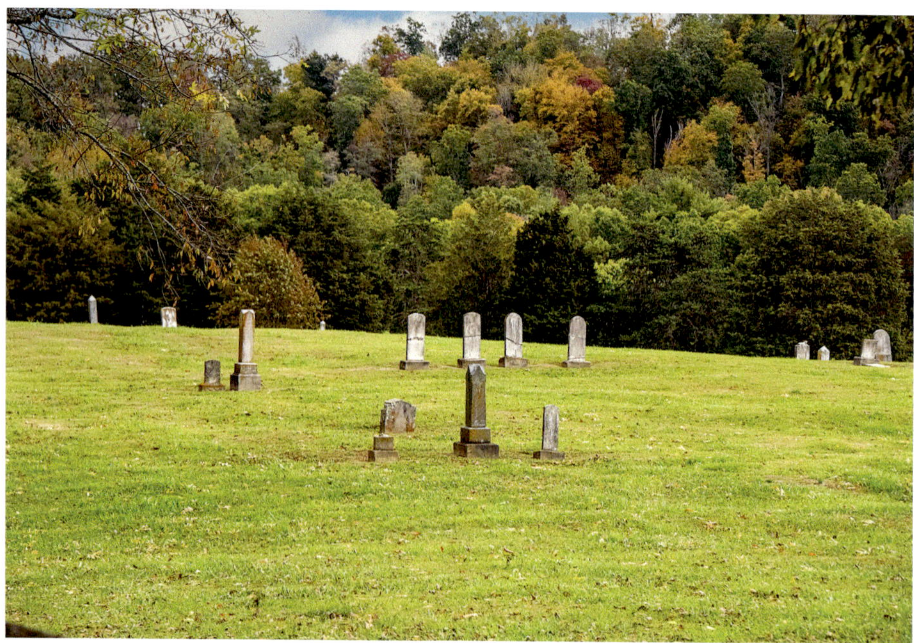

Sparsely marked cemeteries may look empty, but many of the graves remain unmarked due to age, degrading markers, and passing from living memory. The materials used may have been wooden markers or stone that did not hold up under weather and time.

A certain identity began to be associated with the Appalachian people, centered around their independence and a sense of place within the mountains. Rugged explorers able to survive without outside help or influence. This fierce independence would play a part in the development of funeral and burial customs all the way down to the stones themselves. They would develop from a limitation of available materials in a region that was monetarily poor. When industry finally poured into the region, that previous circumstance would spur monuments of opulence.

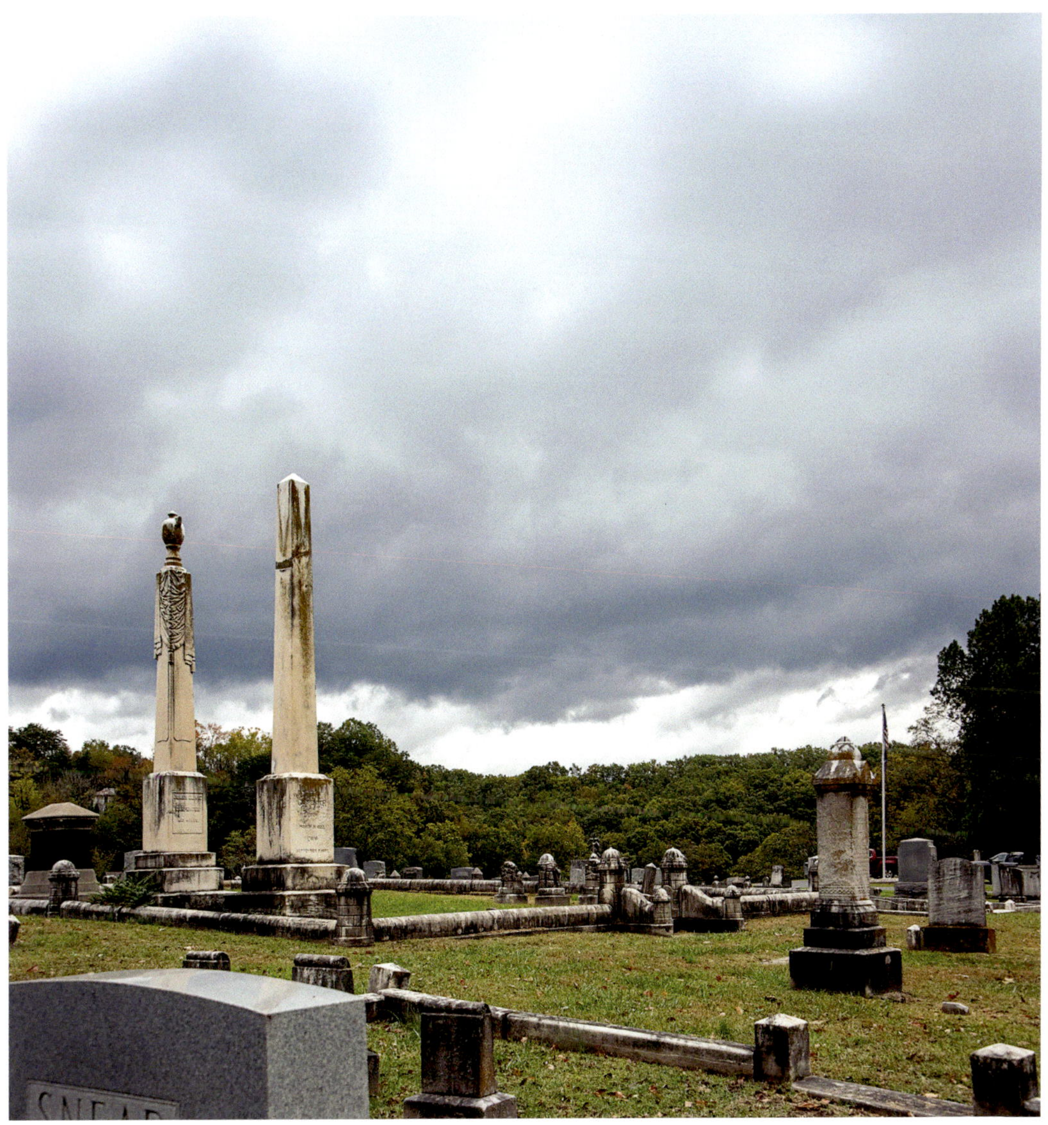

The Industrial Revolution gave way to the rapid growth of Clifton Forge, which was a railway town. Crown Hill Cemetery in the area grew in opulence as a result.

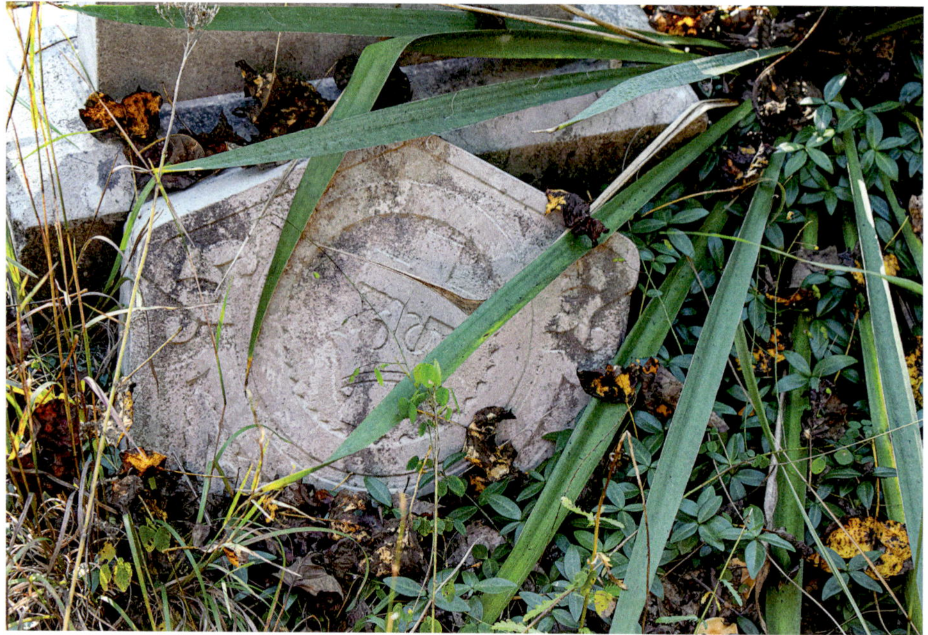

Derelict cemeteries often fall prey to vandalism. McCartney Cemetery in Craig County passed from living memory and now lies mostly untended.

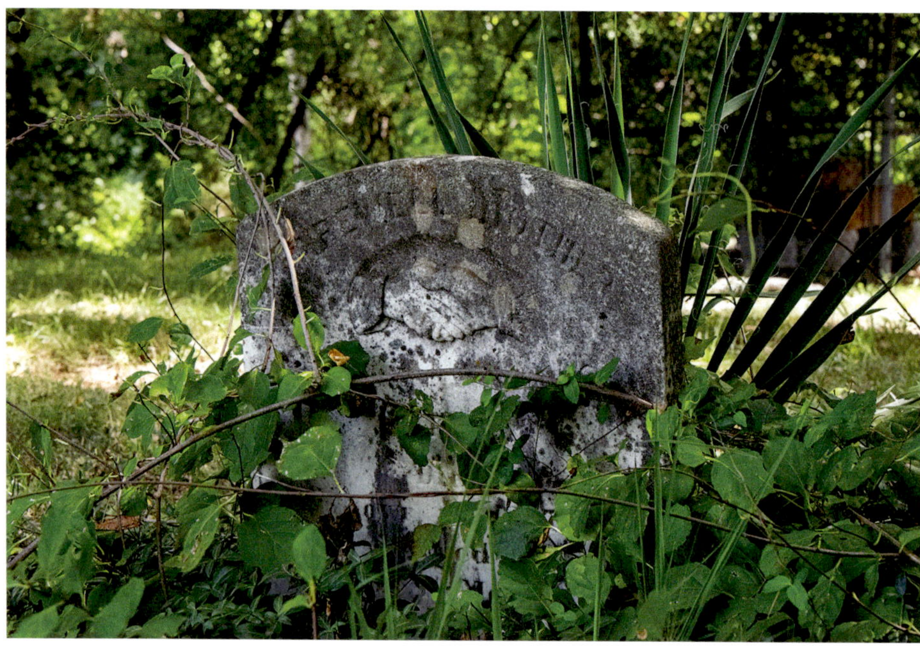

Tombstone Cemetery in Roanoke, Virginia, is loosely maintained with patches that have overgrown. The town has grown in around what was once a more isolated memorial park.

Wars would play a large role in Appalachian pride starting with the Revolutionary War for American Independence. The independence that the mountain people had come to be known for would light the fires of resistance in multiple wars over the centuries. The Revolutionary War would be the first war to call to arms the independent streaks of the men who would come out of the mountains to rise to the cause. This pride would become a calling that would recur during the War of 1812 and again during the Civil War.

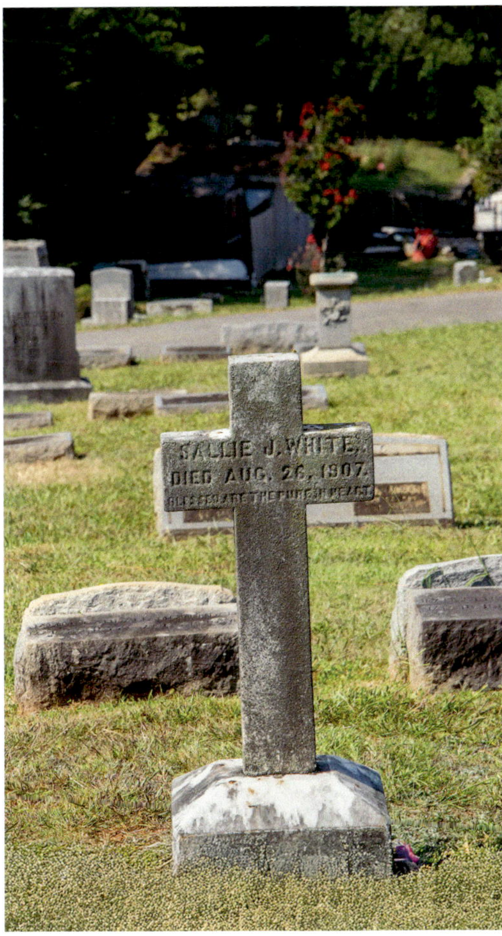

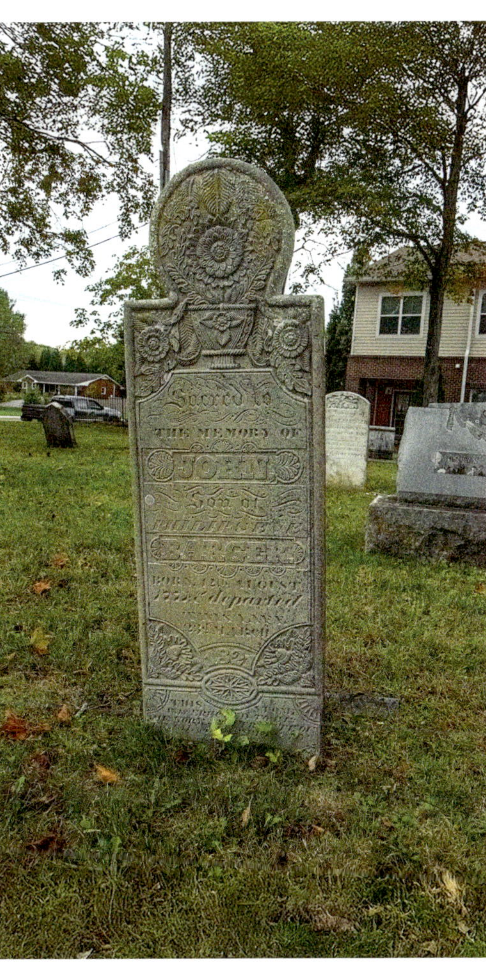

Above left: Simple tombstones marked a time when the more elaborate stones were no feasible. Markers were often made at home. Maintenance in cemeteries often remounts them to preserve them. East Hill Cemetery, Salem, Virginia.

Above right: Opulent stones were rare before the Industrial Revolution in the region. Families of great acclaim or wealth could have them brought in from afar. Barger Cemetery, Blacksburg, Virginia, is maintained voluntarily by John Dudding, who took it on to preserve the site with his own time and money. There is not much known about the family today, only the stones they left behind.

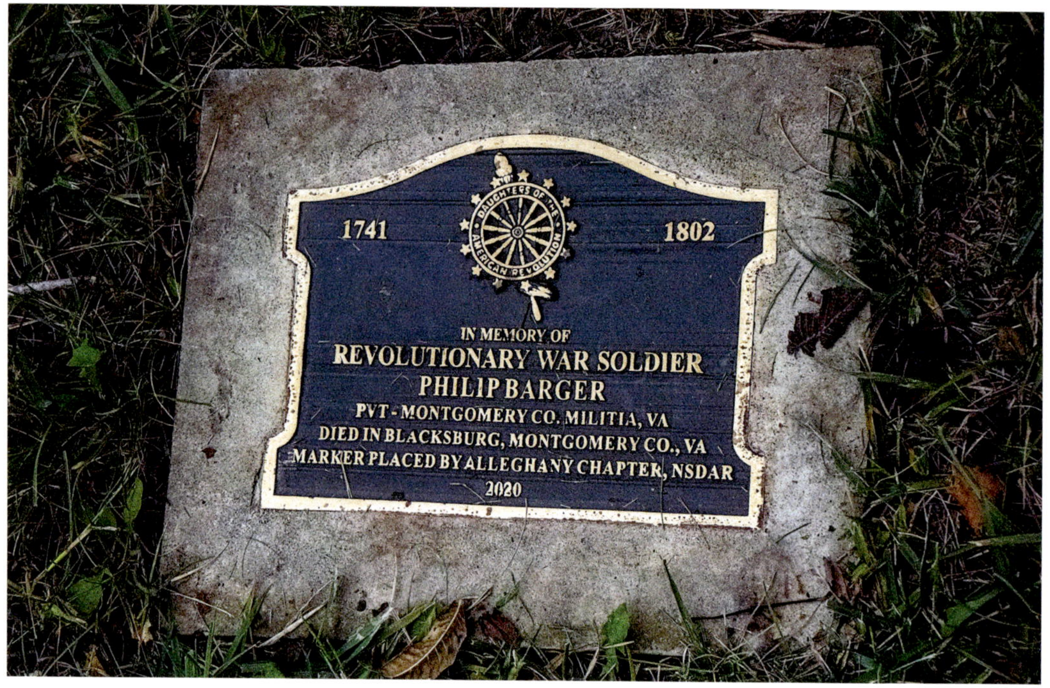

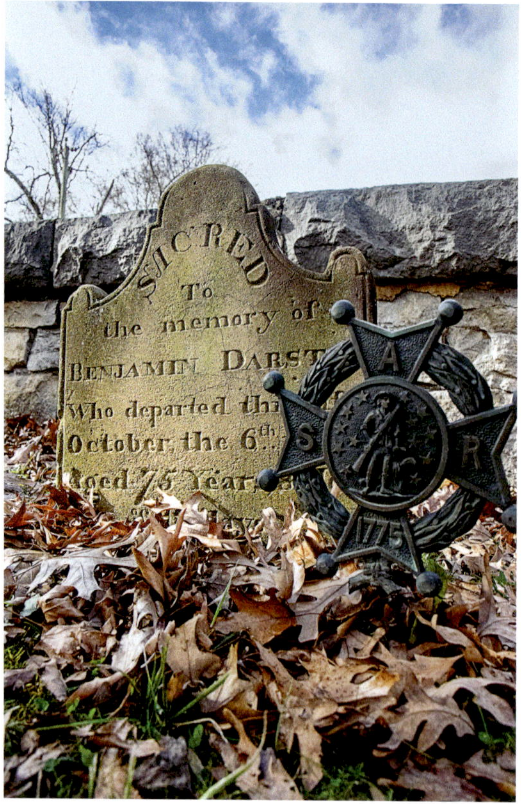

Above: Philip Barger's memorial for his duty as a Revolutionary War soldier in the Montgomery County Militia.

Left: Benjamin Darst: A noted architect and builder as well as a master potter in Lexington who left behind several landmark structures and was a Revolutionary War soldier. His family emigrated from Switzerland in the 1700s.

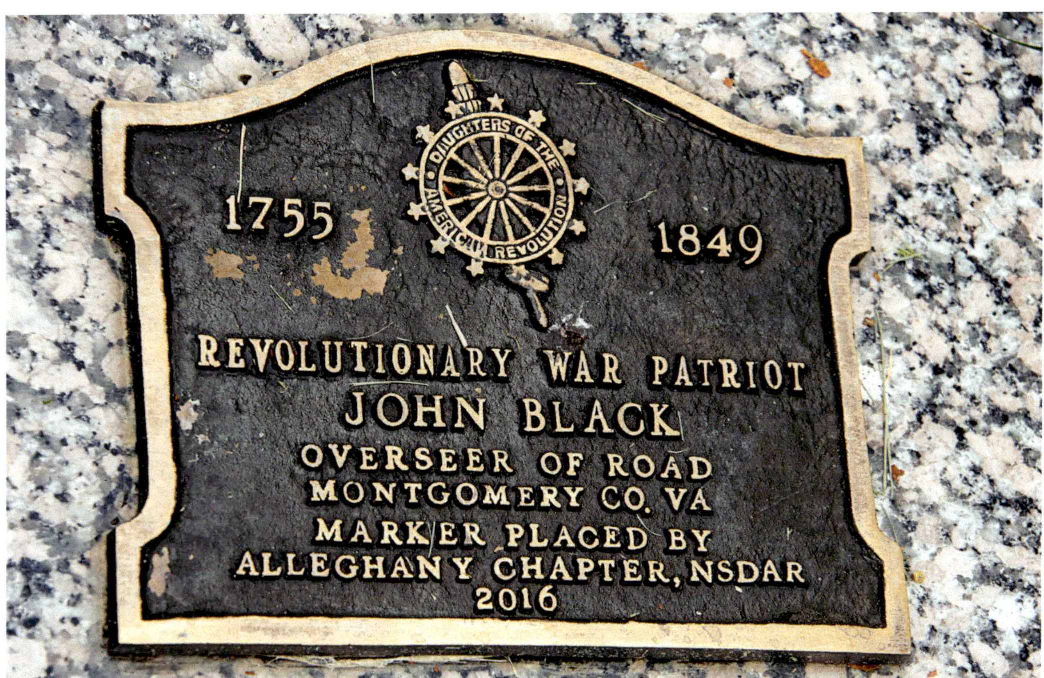

Above: John Black, a Revolutionary War patriot, is interred at Westview Cemetery in Blacksburg, Virginia.

Right: Andrew Moore was a lawyer and politician who studied law under George Wythe. He was a captain in the Continental Army during the American Revolutionary War and was in the battle of Saratoga. He also served in the U.S. Congress and Senate, was a commissioned brigadier general, and a major general of the Virginia Militia. He also was a delegate to the Virginia convention that ratified the federal constitution in 1788.

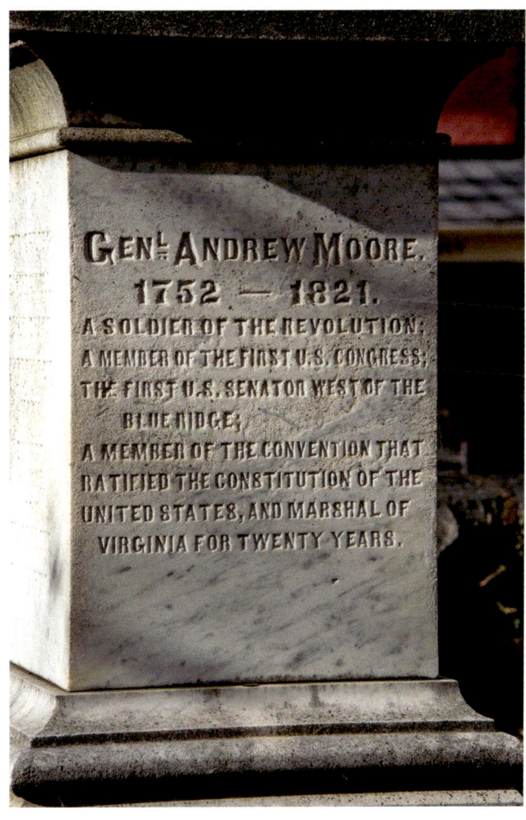

Revolutionary graves abound in the small historic towns of the area. All of the Americans of 1776 were either immigrants or descended from immigrants. The largest group was from England, the second largest were slaves from continental Africa, and the rest came from continental Europe. Particularly Irish and Scottish, which are heavily reflected in the notations on stones denoting lineage.

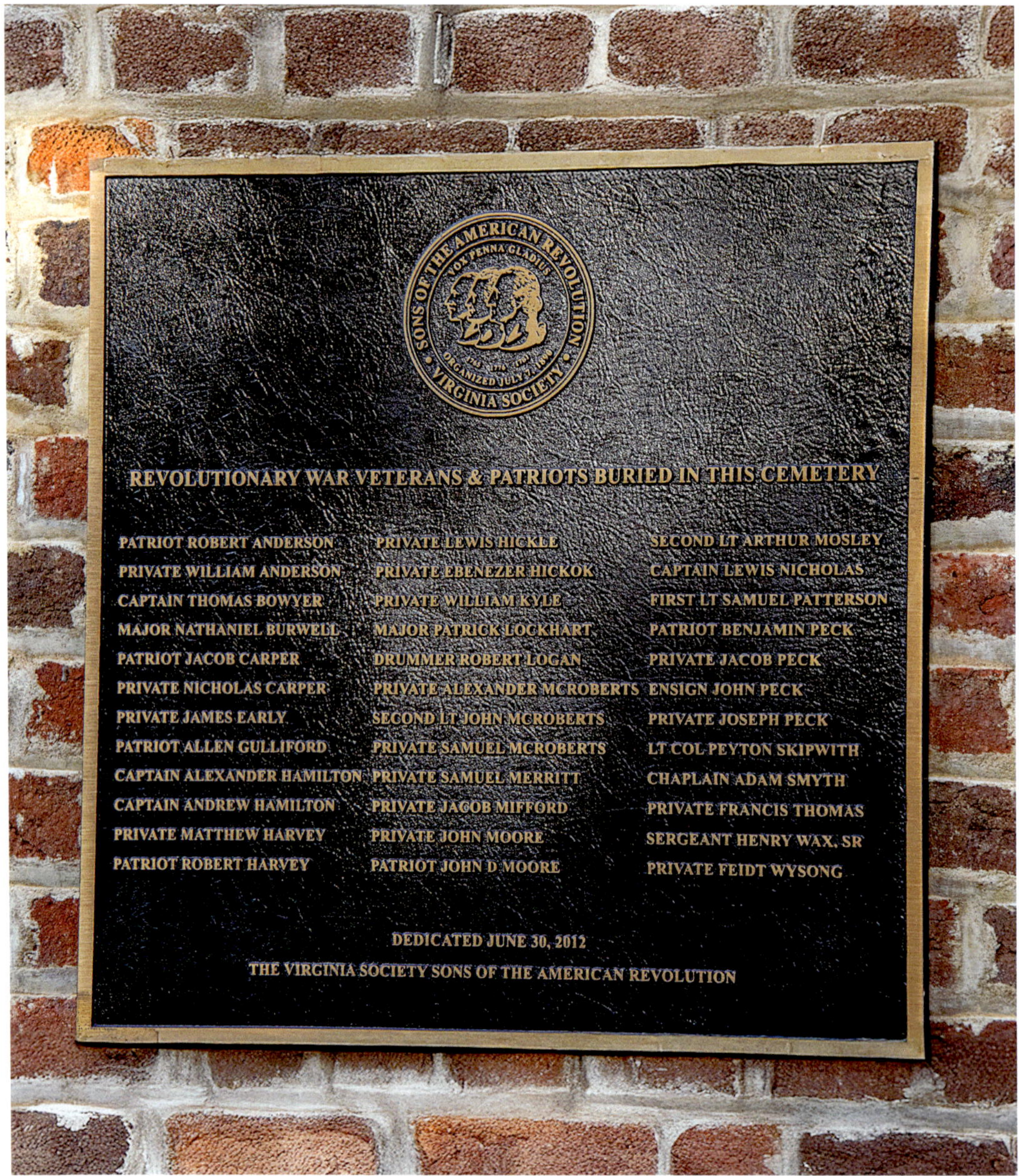

At the Fincastle Presbyterian Church, there is a memorial plaque representing the known Revolutionary War veterans in the graveyard. Few, if any, of their stones remain.

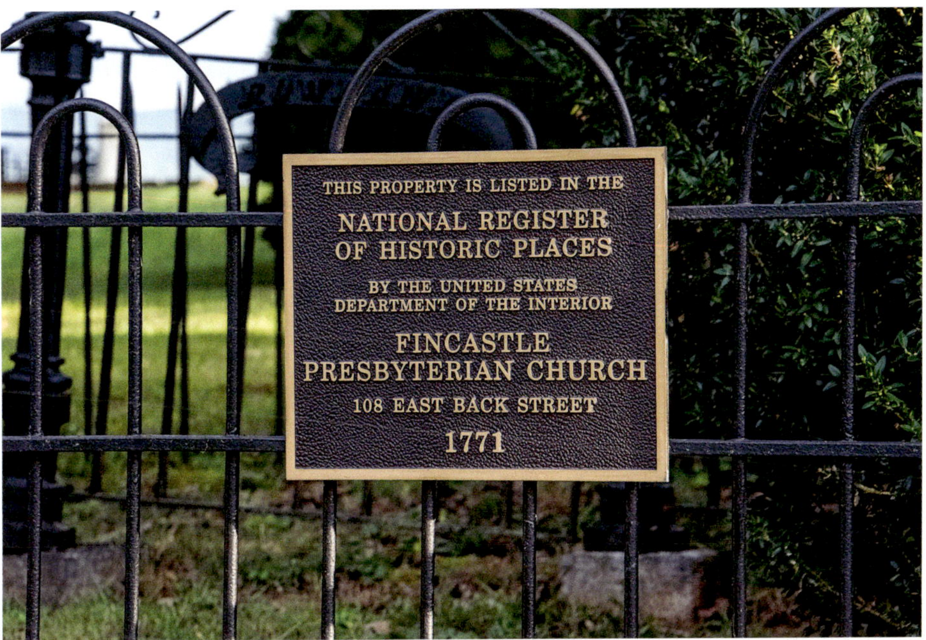

Historic marker for one of the oldest cemeteries in Southwest Virginia. Fincastle Presbyterian Church is on the National Register of Historic Places.

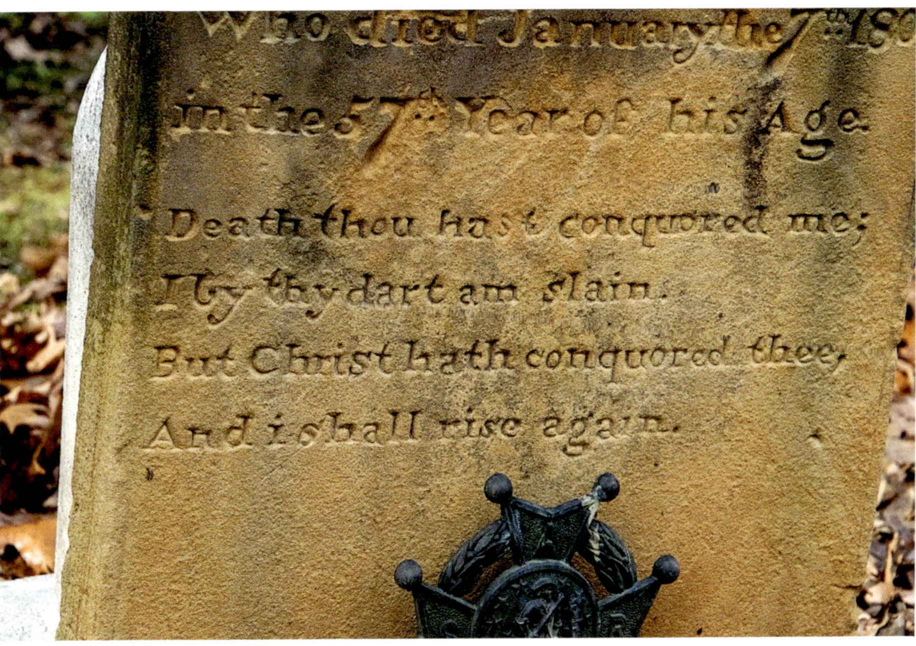

A Revolutionary War veteran's stone epithet located in Oak Grove Cemetery in Lexington, Virginia.

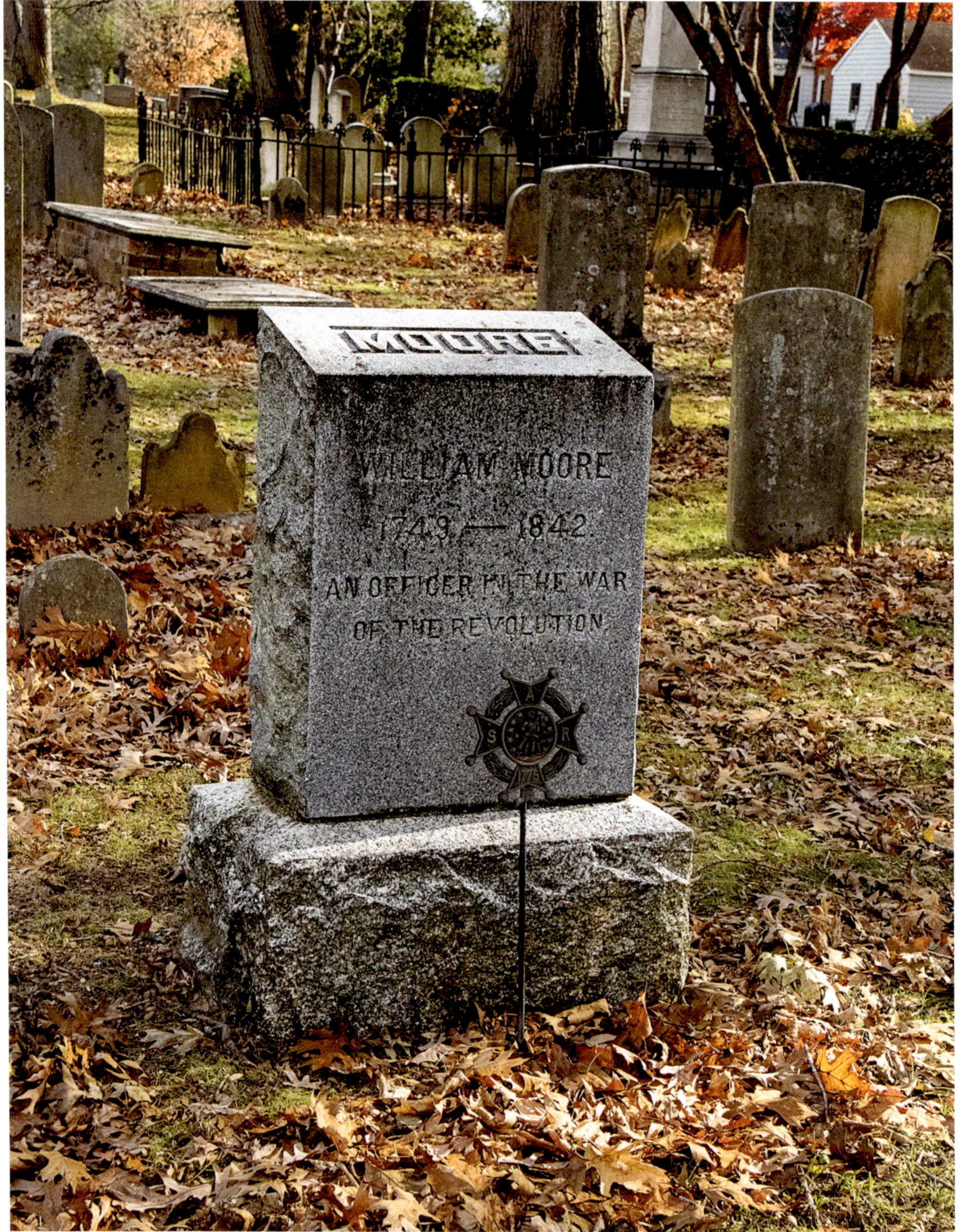

William Moore was well known for his physical strength and temperate nature. He was in military service during the entirety of the Revolutionary War and held the rank of captain. He was present at the surrender of Cornwallis. After the war, he settled in Lexington as a merchant. Captain Moore established an iron furnace on the South River and then was a justice of the peace and a high sheriff for two terms.

After the Revolutionary War, there was heavy migration to Appalachia. Land was granted to veterans after Native people were removed by the Washington Administration. After this influx, those who rose to leadership dubbed this region as separate from the rest of civilization and declared their society as Choee. The meaning of the word is "champion of the oppressed" and would later also become a surname. The society that had developed was mostly defined by ranching, farming, and fur trading (this was before coal and iron ore deposits were discovered). They varied in religion and most of the dialect of Appalachia developed out of Scottish-Irish. These developments created the identity that is the basis of the regional boundaries seen today.

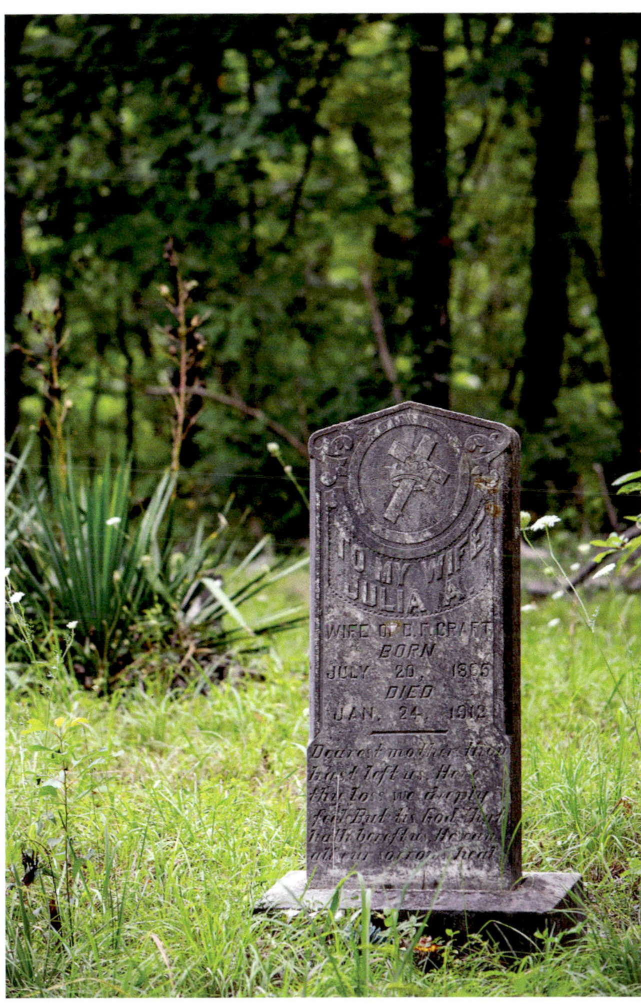

Located in McCartney Cemetery is a beautifully carved stone to a mother.

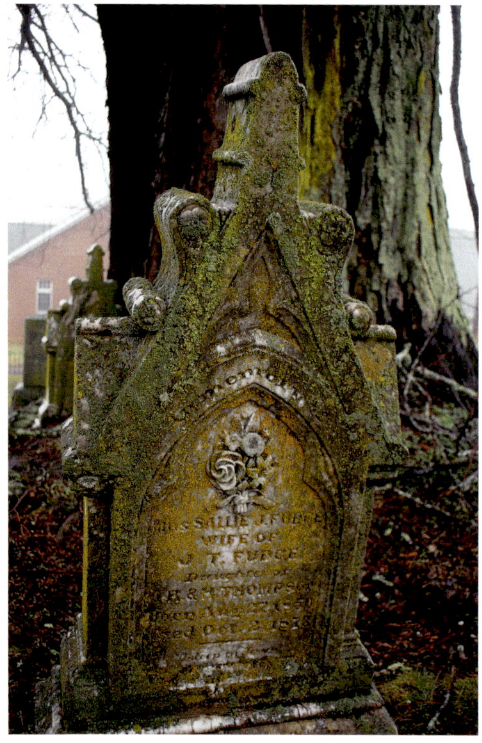

Located in Goodwin Cemetery, Fincastle, Virginia, is a very ornate Victorian stone. The symbolism of a full rose for an adult, morning glory for mortality and farewell, a daffodil for beauty and deep regard.

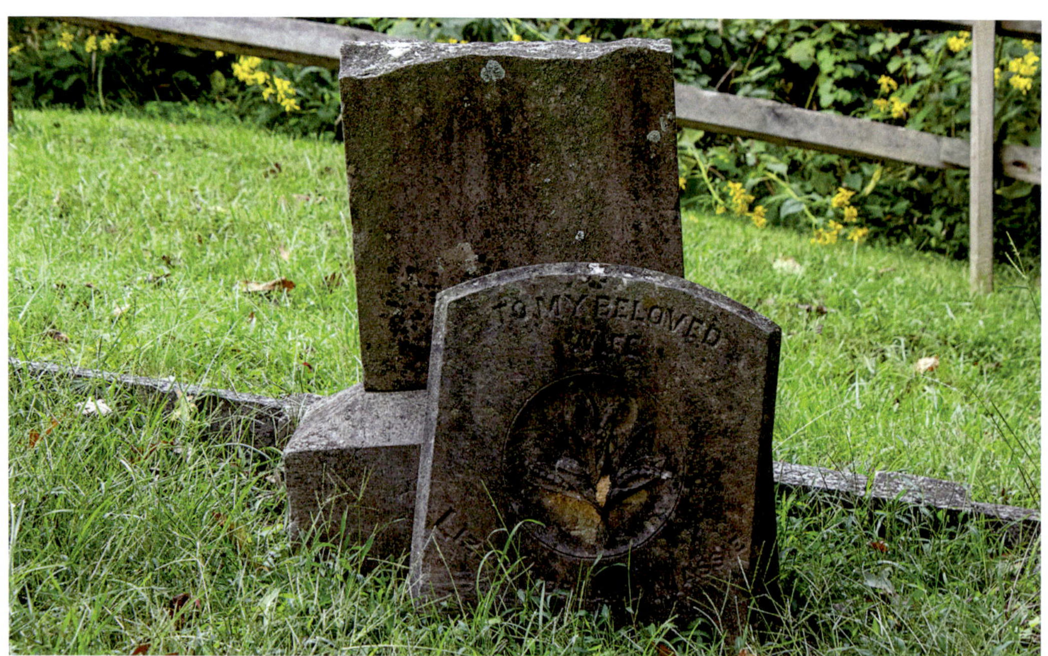

Closed mountain cemetery in Botetourt, Virginia, on a historic site. The sweet pea on the stone would suggest a child.

The discovery of coal and iron deposits would begin the outside influences into what had, up to this point, been a very introverted society that shunned outsiders. This would bring roads, trains, and society to the region. This is reflected in the older cemeteries. As you walk among the stones, there is a clear divide between the classes. It is reflected in the materials, craftsmanship, size and number of the monuments, with a few distinct exceptions.

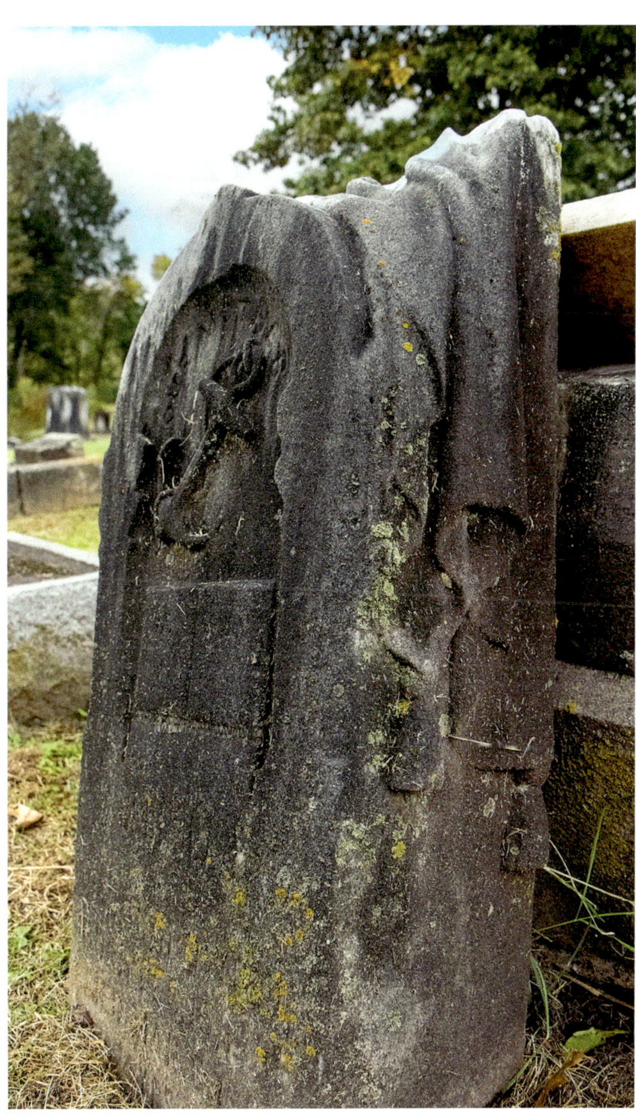

Stone from the areas where iron ore and other minerals were mined are common in the region because they were the places where the departed worked. This one has worn quickly to only the carved symbols. An anchor had many meanings, but, generally, it was to convey a meaning of enduring hope and faith in the afterlife. The mourning cloth with tassels were the veil between life and death.

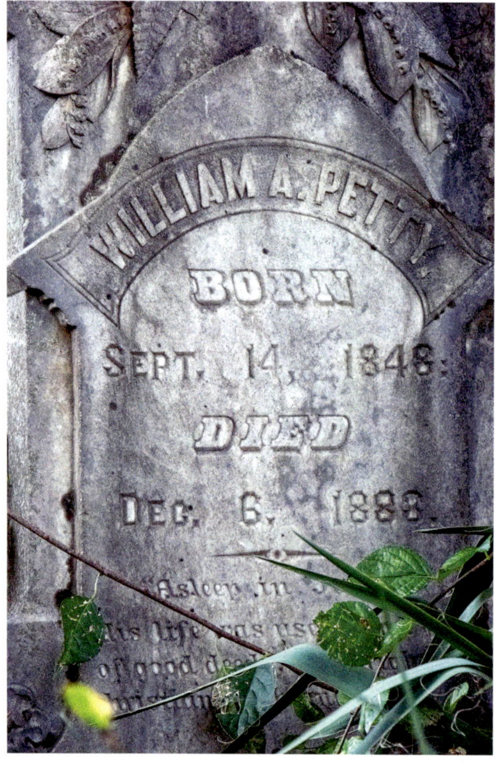

Ornately carved marker located in Tombstone Cemetery, Roanoke, Virginia.

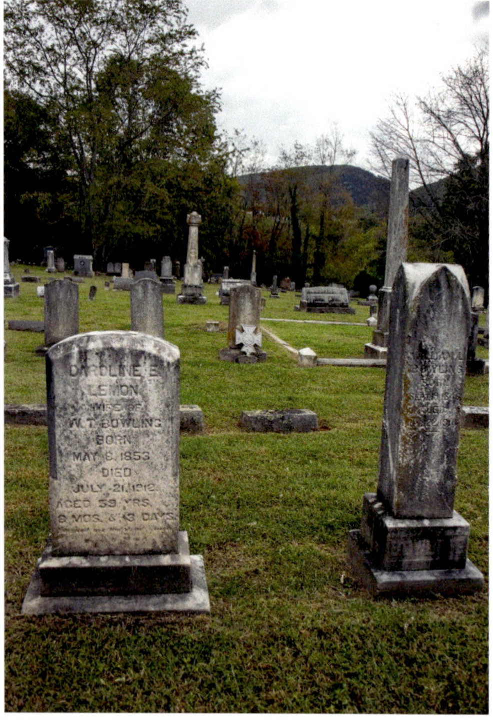

Stones in the Crown Hill Cemetery, Clifton Forge, Virginia. Many larger cemeteries are located on mountain landscapes, making for challenging burials.

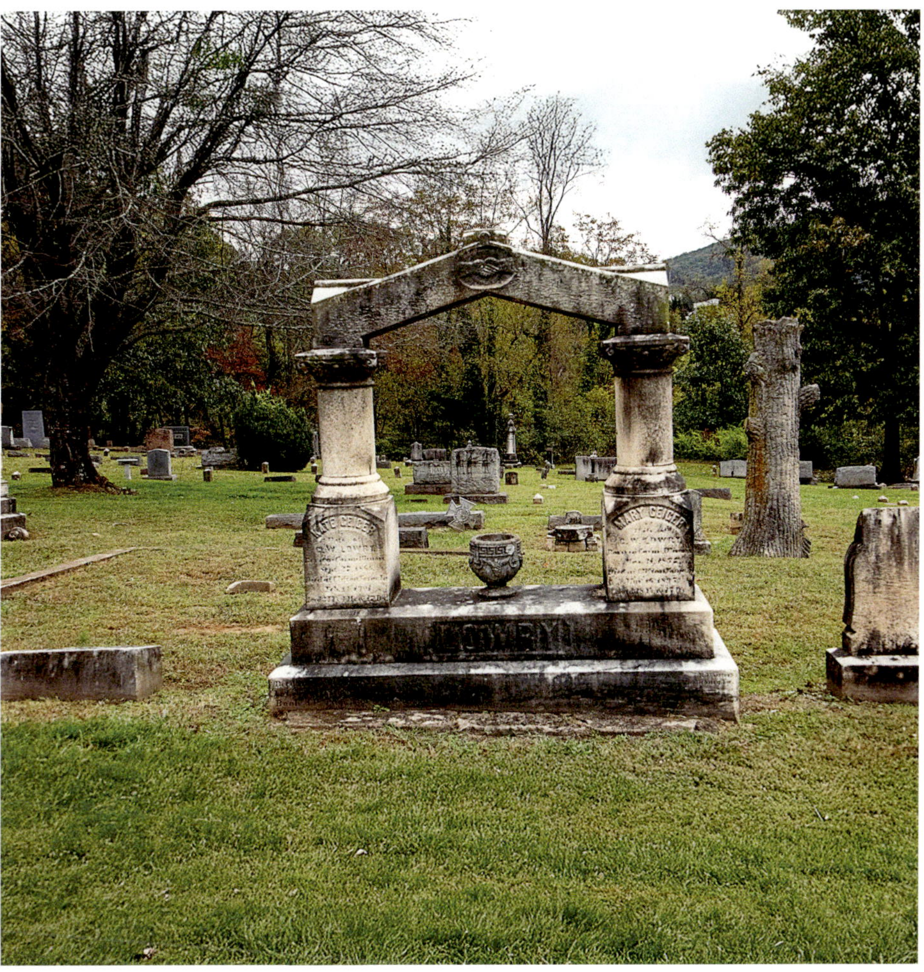

Sisters buried at Crown Hill Cemetery, Clifton Forge, Virginia. The clasped hands have many meanings, so subtle differences such as sleeve cuffs or orientation are determinate of the meaning. In this case, with the clasped hands between them, it represents sisters.

Nearly every small mountain cemetery has at least one monument that is out of place in an otherwise uniformly simple cemetery. It whispers of a heart-wrenching loss reflected in the care to create a memorial that stands apart. Most of the stories of these incredible pieces are lost to time, therefore leaving the sad tale to the imagination.

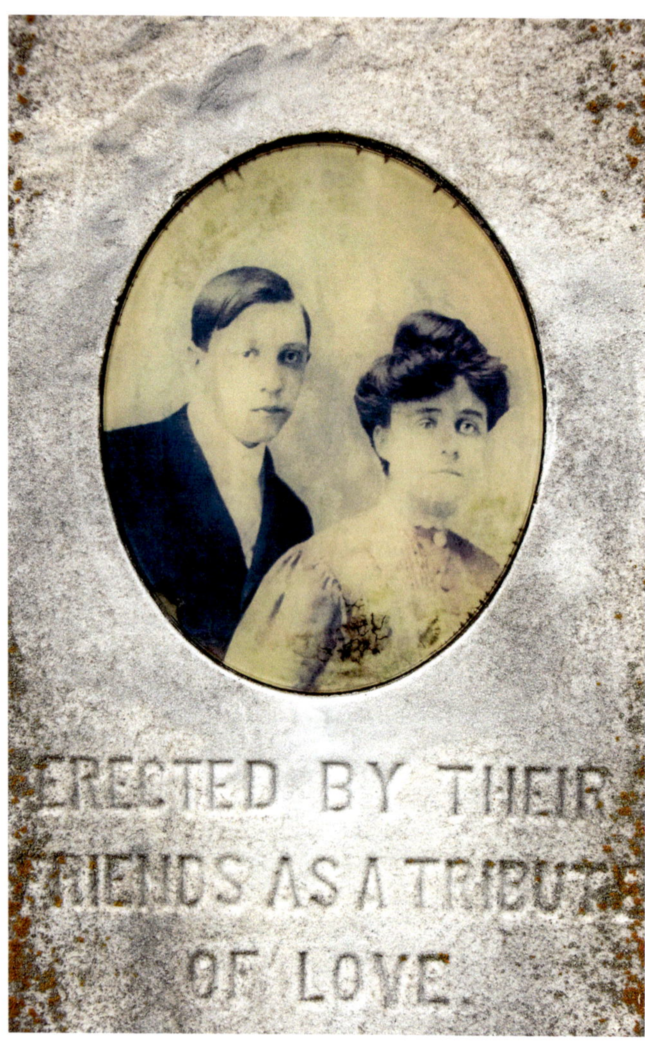

Crown Hill Cemetery, Clifton Forge, Virginia. Mabel Pendleton, eighteen, and Stuart Gay, sixteen, were making their third attempt to elope. Stuart's father, a C&O conductor, learned of the plan and sought to intercept. In desperation, Mabel jumped from a footbridge and Stuart followed. They fell 40 feet into the Jackson River and subsequently drowned in 10 feet of water.

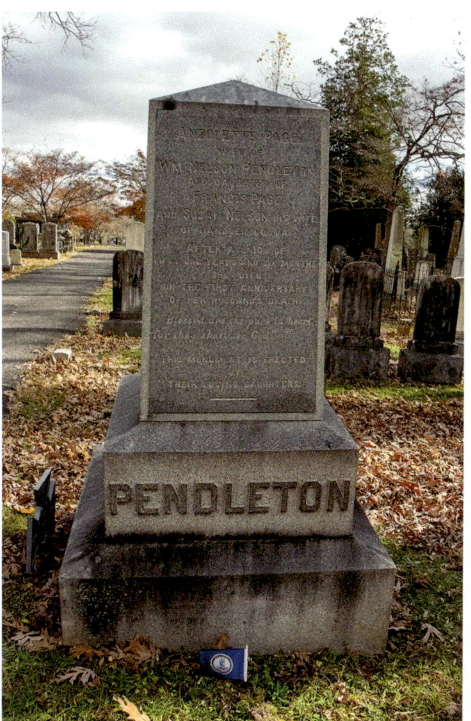

Anzolette Page Pendleton, wife of William Nelson Pendleton. They were married for fifty-one years and six months. She died on the first anniversary of her husband's death. Oak Grove Cemetery, Lexington, Virginia.

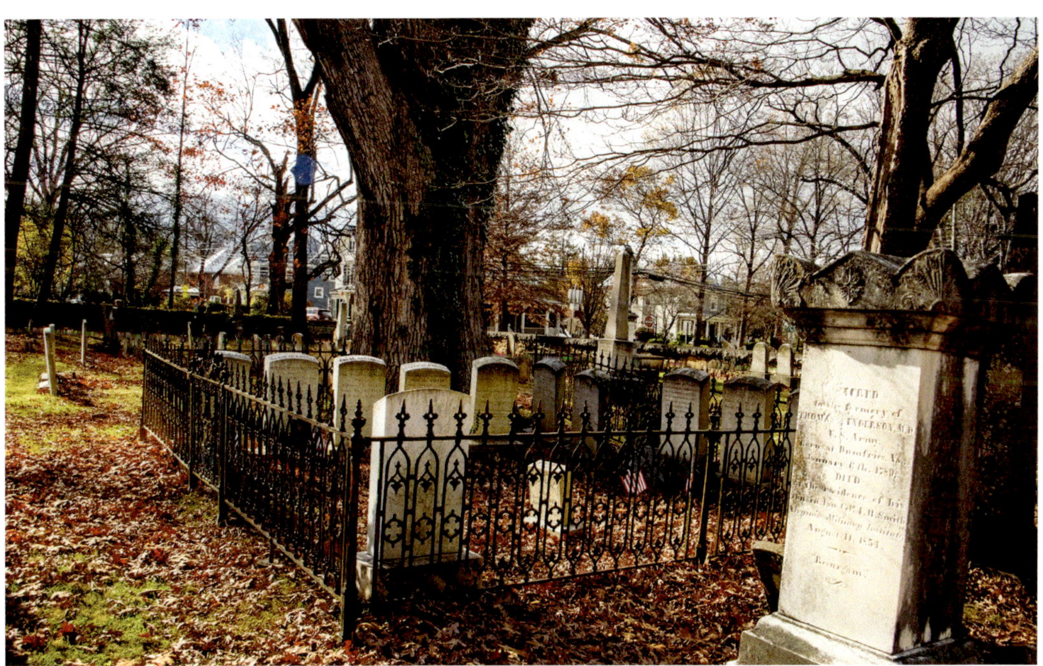

Class separation in the plots divided by wrought-iron fencing and quality of stones and carvings, Oak Grove Cemetery, Lexington, Virginia.

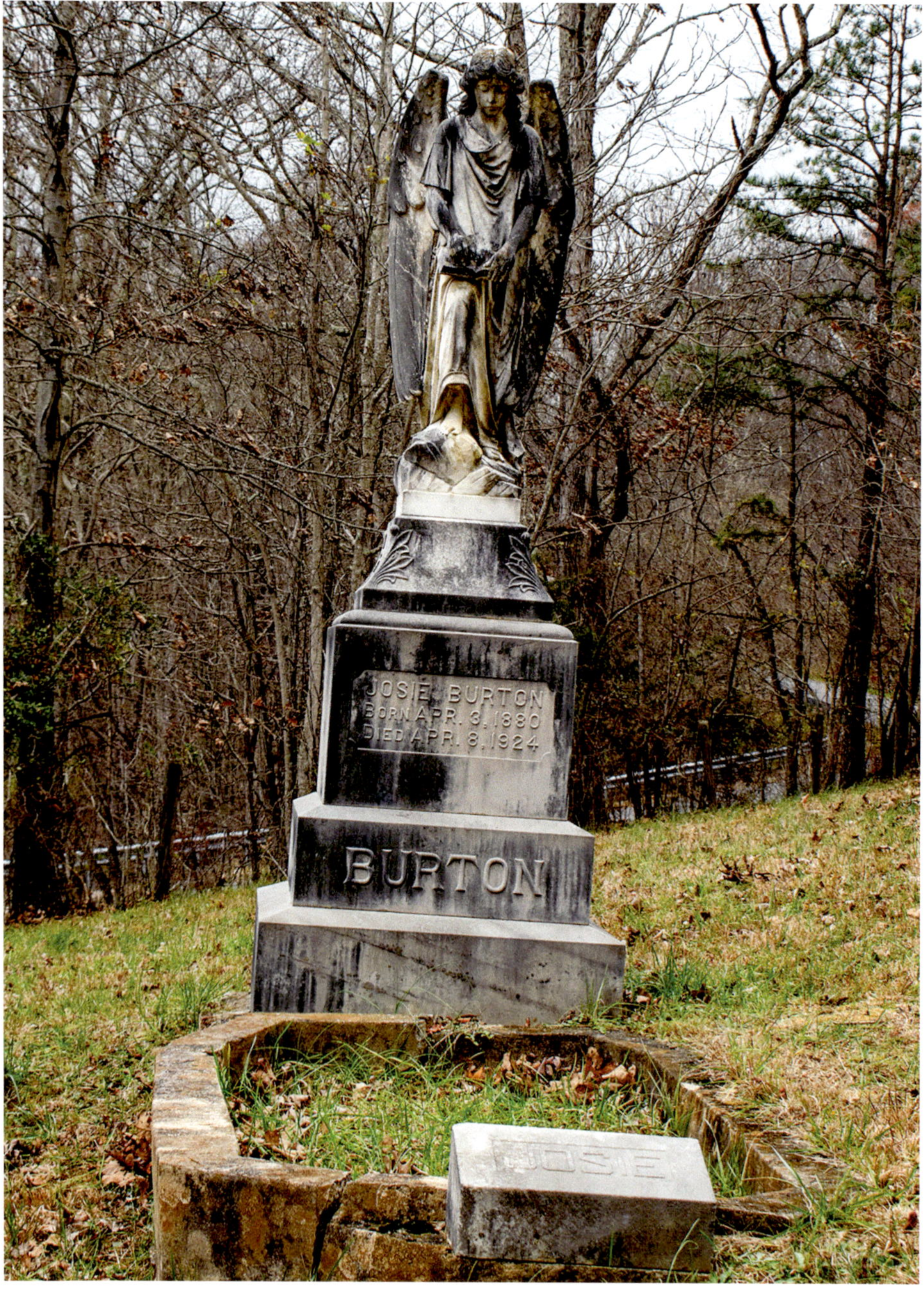

Eggleston, Virginia, grave of Josie Burton. This is the only large grave marker in an otherwise very plain mountain cemetery full of weather worn stones. On the stone is an angel writing in heaven's ledger. The grave also has a stone flower bed and footstone, as well as a detailed inscription on the back. The story behind the devotion of Josie is lost to time as it has passed from living memory.

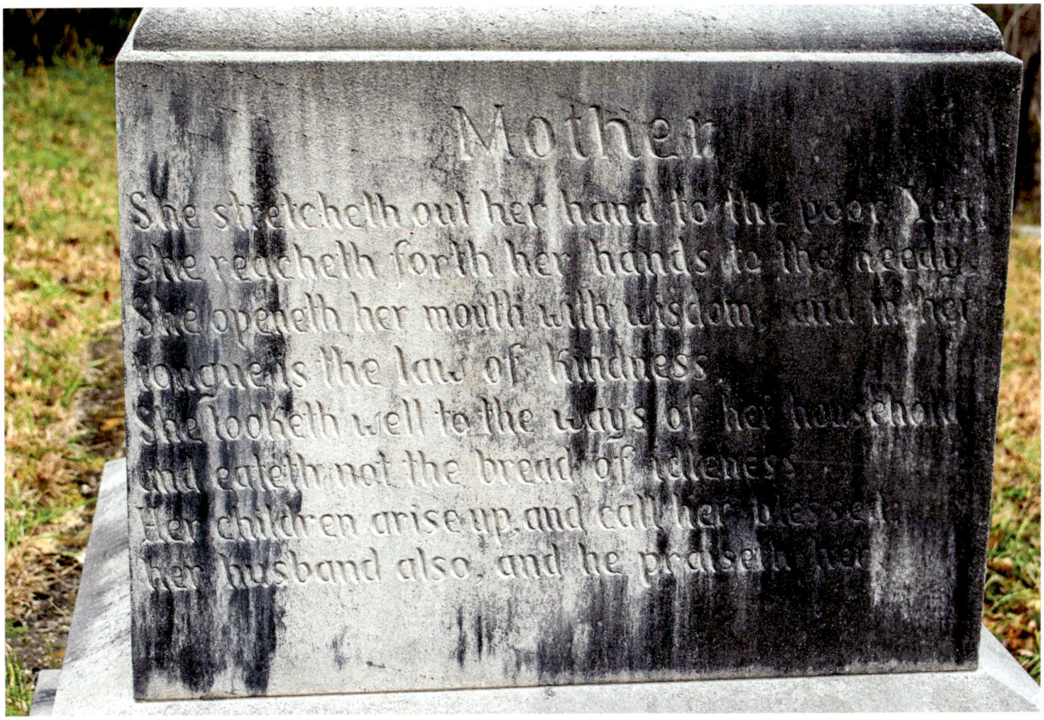

Above: Dedication of undying love for a mother by her family. The inscription is on the back side of the angel statue, Eggleston, Virginia.

Right: World War II stones are not uncommon in the region; however, a female officer from that era is a special find. Tombstone Cemetery, Roanoke, Virginia.

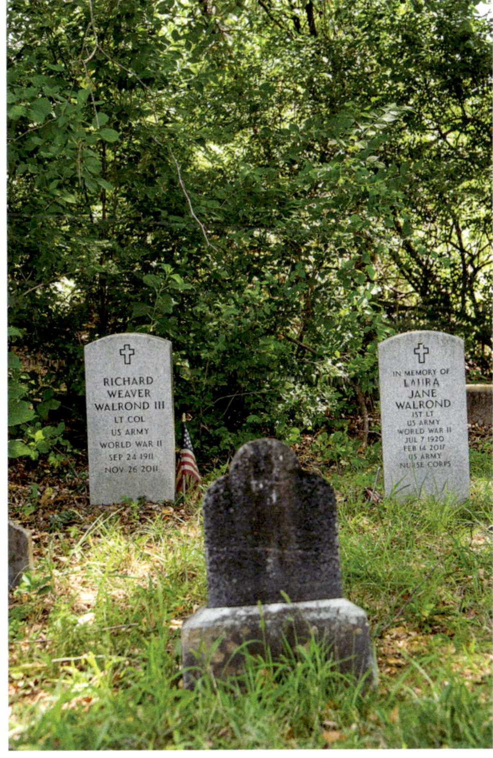

This divide from the rest of the culture that developed outside of the Choee region would come to a pinnacle when the Civil War broke out. It is very evident throughout the cemeteries where, even today, the graves are often clearly marked. Opposing sides are buried side by side. One of the most poignant things about the long-standing cemeteries is the layers within. From colonist to settlers to the Revolutionary War, the War of 1812, the Civil War, and everything in-between. It mirrors not only the times in which the burials took place, but the layers of the lives that existed in the dash between the date of birth and the date of death of the decedents.

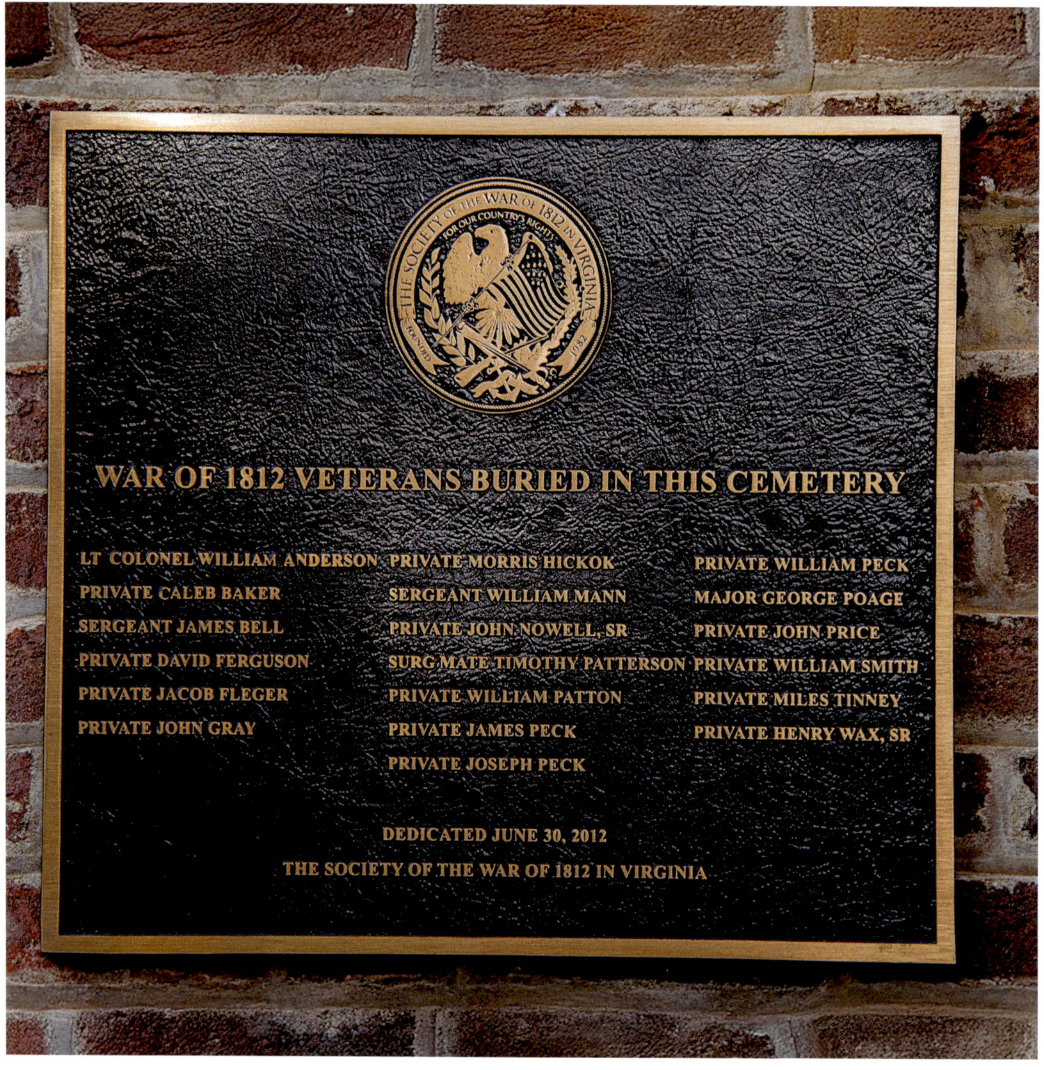

Patriotism is strong in the region. In every cemetery, there are graves of war, but few that have as many patriot soldiers as Fincastle Presbyterian Cemetery (graveyard). The Revolutionary War, the War of 1812, the American Civil War, World War I, and World War II are heavily represented.

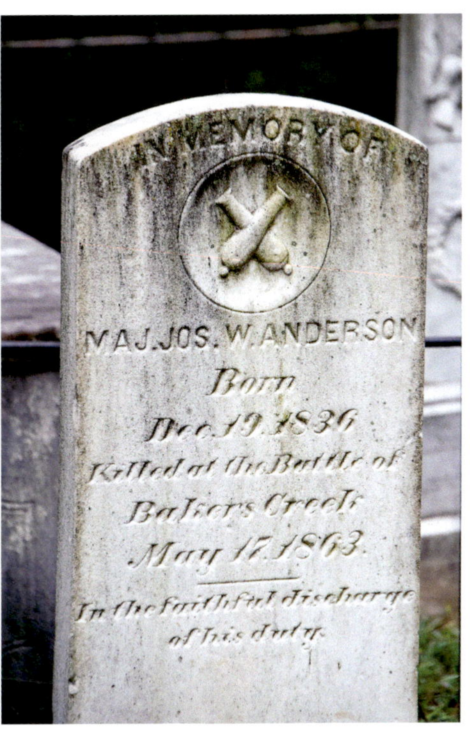

Right: Major Anderson was a graduate of University of Virginia, a lawyer, and plantation owner. He was elected a lieutenant in the militia, and when the Civil War broke out, he was elevated to captain. At the battle of Champion Hill (Baker's Creek), he was shot from his horse attempting to rally Barton's retreating soldiers. He is buried at Fincastle Presbyterian Cemetery and there is a national park installation for him at Vicksburg.

Below: World War I and II plaque honoring those in the cemetery of the Fincastle Presbyterian Cemetery, Virginia.

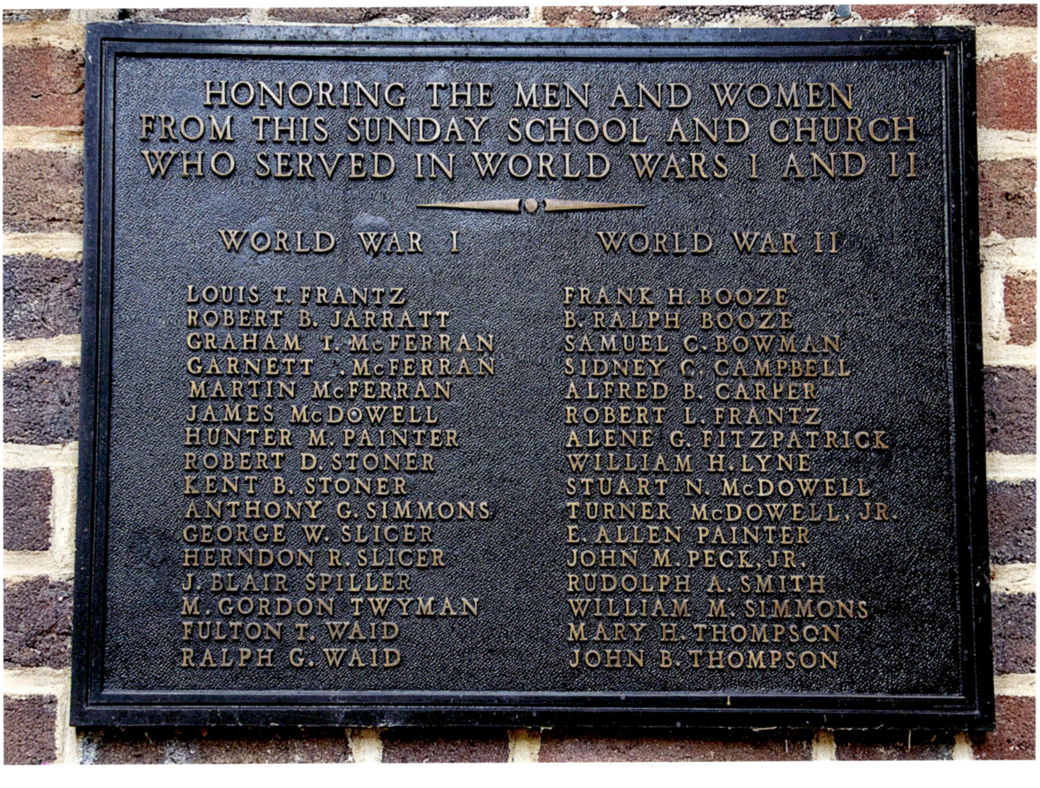

HONORING THE MEN AND WOMEN
FROM THIS SUNDAY SCHOOL AND CHURCH
WHO SERVED IN WORLD WARS I AND II

WORLD WAR I	WORLD WAR II
LOUIS T. FRANTZ	FRANK H. BOOZE
ROBERT B. JARRATT	B. RALPH BOOZE
GRAHAM T. McFERRAN	SAMUEL C. BOWMAN
GARNETT .McFERRAN	SIDNEY C. CAMPBELL
MARTIN McFERRAN	ALFRED B. CARPER
JAMES McDOWELL	ROBERT L. FRANTZ
HUNTER M. PAINTER	ALENE G. FITZPATRICK
ROBERT D. STONER	WILLIAM H. LYNE
KENT B. STONER	STUART N. McDOWELL
ANTHONY G. SIMMONS	TURNER McDOWELL, JR.
GEORGE W. SLICER	E. ALLEN PAINTER
HERNDON R. SLICER	JOHN M. PECK, JR.
J. BLAIR SPILLER	RUDOLPH A. SMITH
M. GORDON TWYMAN	WILLIAM M. SIMMONS
FULTON T. WAID	MARY H. THOMPSON
RALPH G. WAID	JOHN B. THOMPSON

Many gravestones reflect evidence of the lives lived. The symbolism behind the carvings can mean anything from one's convictions to religious beliefs, passions, vocation, family lineage, or culture. Some stones are so weather worn that the occupants of their graves are lost to time forever. Others are carved of stone that has stood up to the elements. The occupants of many have long passed living memory, and they now go unvisited. Entire cemeteries that have passed the memory barrier fall into disrepair and are abandoned to the elements. The ornate ones catch the eye and the imagination.

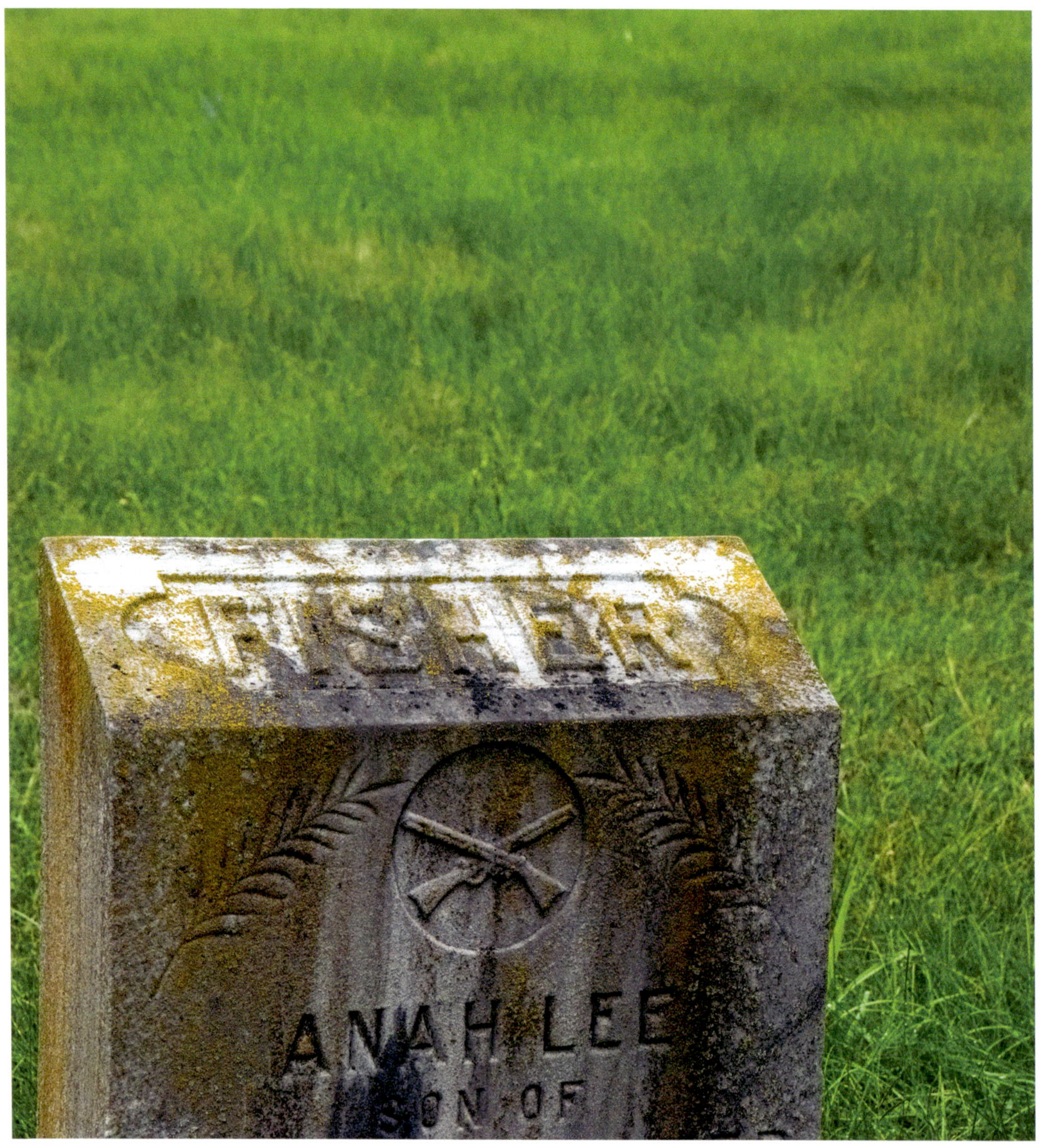

Crossed rifles are a symbol a death that occurred during service (usually in war). This one is located on a marker in Locust Bottom Cemetery, Botetourt, Virginia.

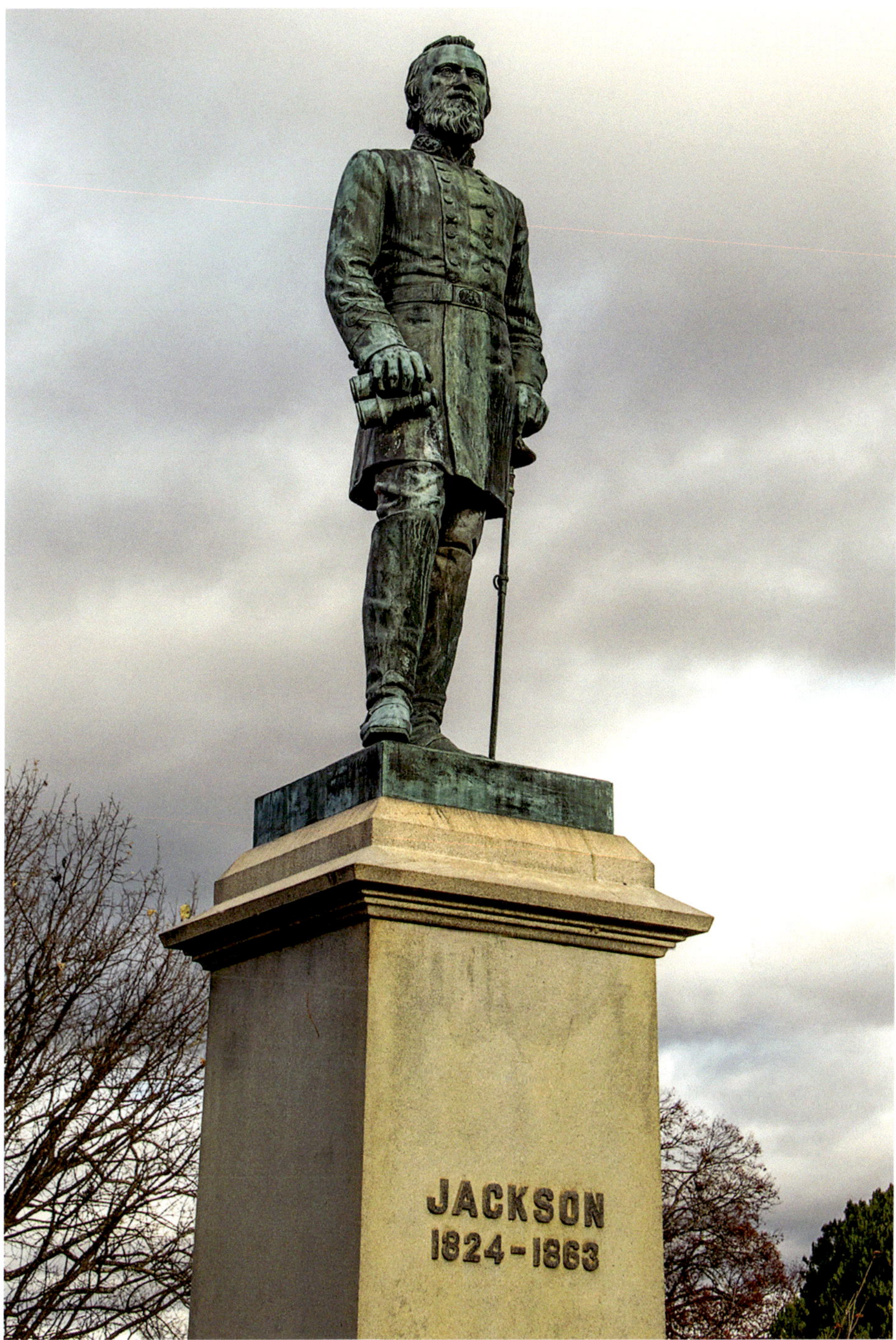

The Stonewall Jackson monument in Oak Grove Cemetery, Lexington, Virginia, was erected in the 1940s and the occupants of his family plot were moved to be placed under the monument. His given name was Thomas Jonathan Jackson. Born an orphan, he rose to fame as one of the most valued generals in the Confederate Army.

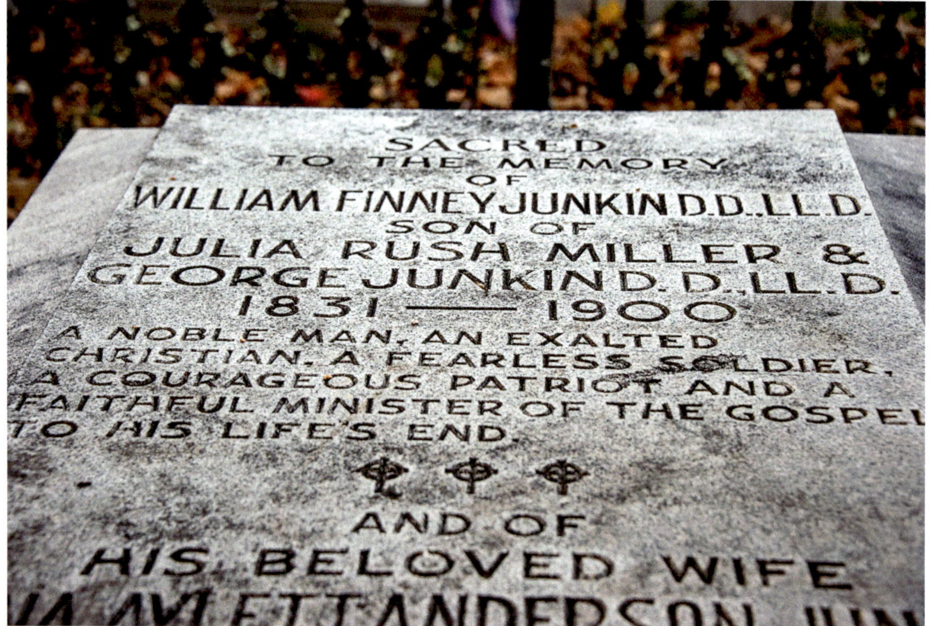

The stone detailing the virtues of William Finney Junkin, Oak Grove Cemetery, Lexington, Virginia.

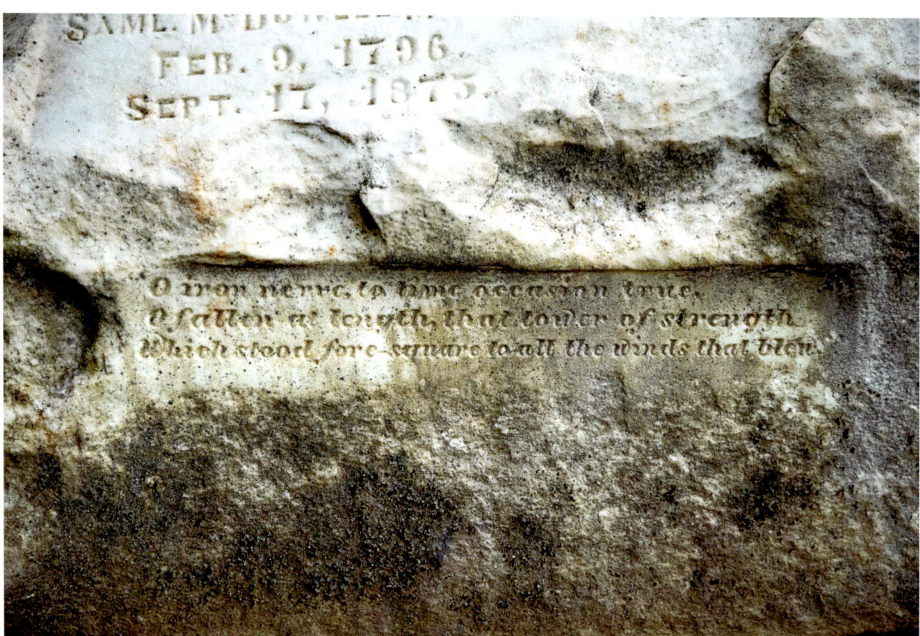

Samuel McDowell Moore's epitaph, Oak Grove Cemetery, Lexington, Virginia. It reads "O iron nerve to true occasion true, O fallen at length that tower of strength. Which stood four-square to all the winds that blew!" It is the ode on the death of the duke of Wellington penned by Alfred Tennyson.

Right: Martha Diggs' stone portrays a woman who was socially graceful and loved by the community. She lived during the time of the Revolutionary War and presided over the Rustic Lodge. She was the wife of Captain Nathaniel Burwell of the Virginia Artillery during the Revolutionary War and was the subject of a book, A Girl's Life in Virginia Before the War by Letitia M Burwell. Gravesite is Fincastle Presbyterian Graveyard.

Below: John White Brockenbrough was originally a lawyer who would become the Commonwealth's attorney and then a federal judge of the U.S. District Court. During the Civil War, he served as a member of the Confederate Congress. He was a founder and professor of law for what is now Washington and Lee University. Stone in Oak Grove Cemetery, Lexington, Virginia.

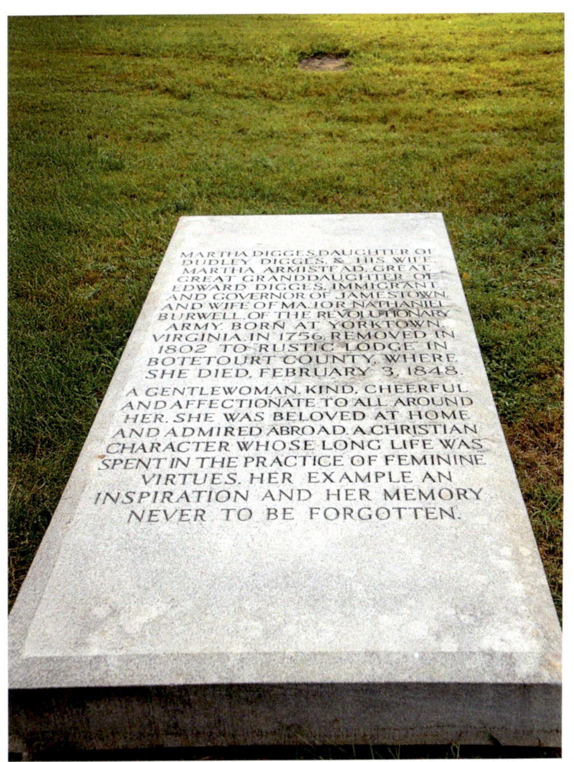

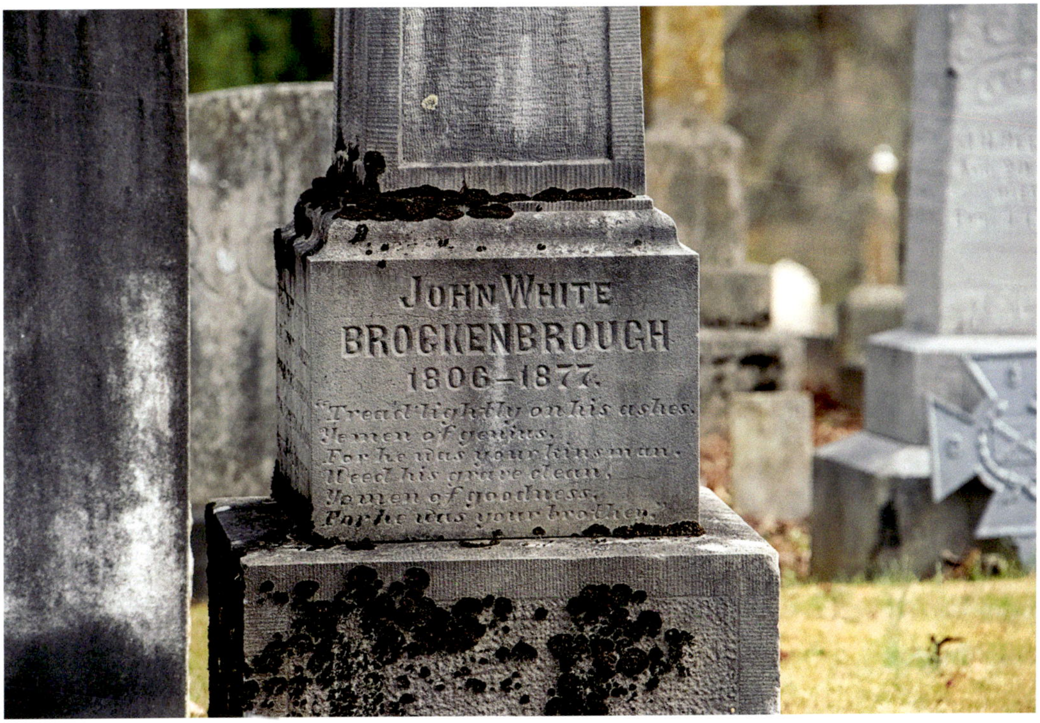

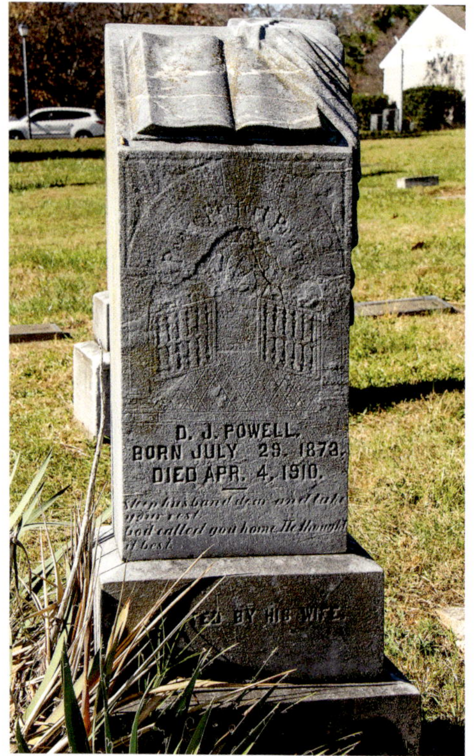

Left: Located in East Hill Cemetery, Salem, Virginia, this stone is a good example of symbolism in cemetery carvings. The work involved in this stone would have been tremendous. The book is the story of his life, only half gone, the mourning cloth draped over the corner of one side. The epitaph of a religious nature and the gates of heaven with a depiction of Jesus on the other side. The words above it, unfortunately lost to weather and time.

Below: Crypts at Hollins University, carefully detailed stones and literary references. Roanoke, VA.

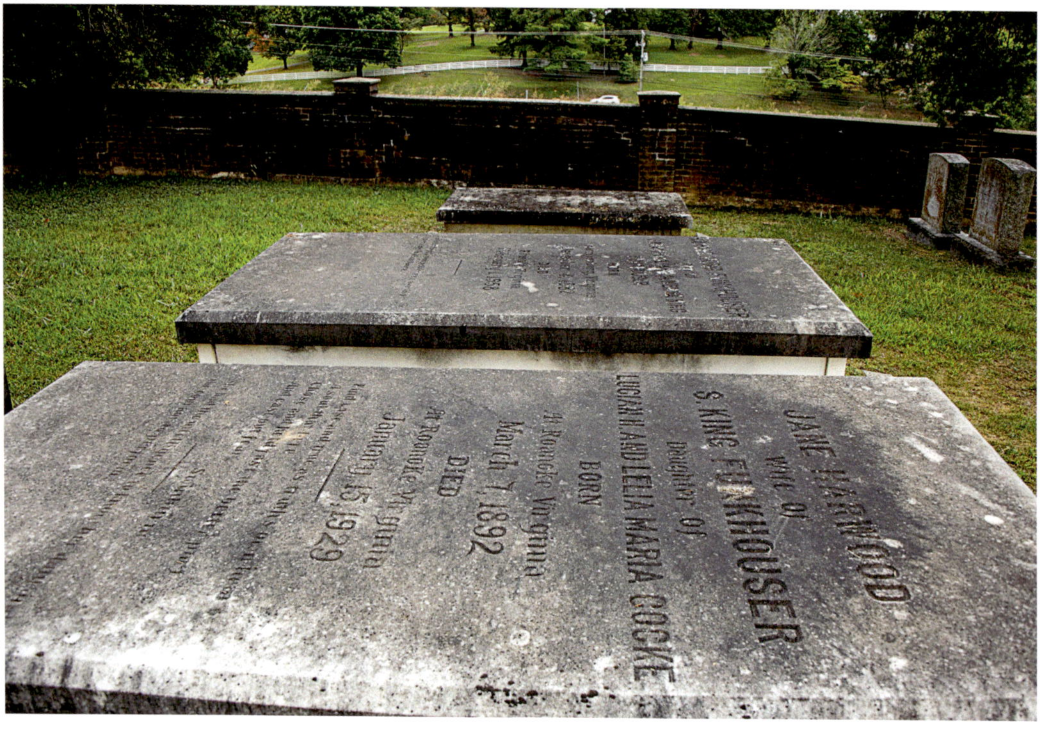

The layers of our nation from birth to present day lay within the hallowed grounds of these places of eternal rest. They tell a story, if you know how to read the stones. The most innocuous symbol of all being the dash, which holds the secrets taken to the grave.

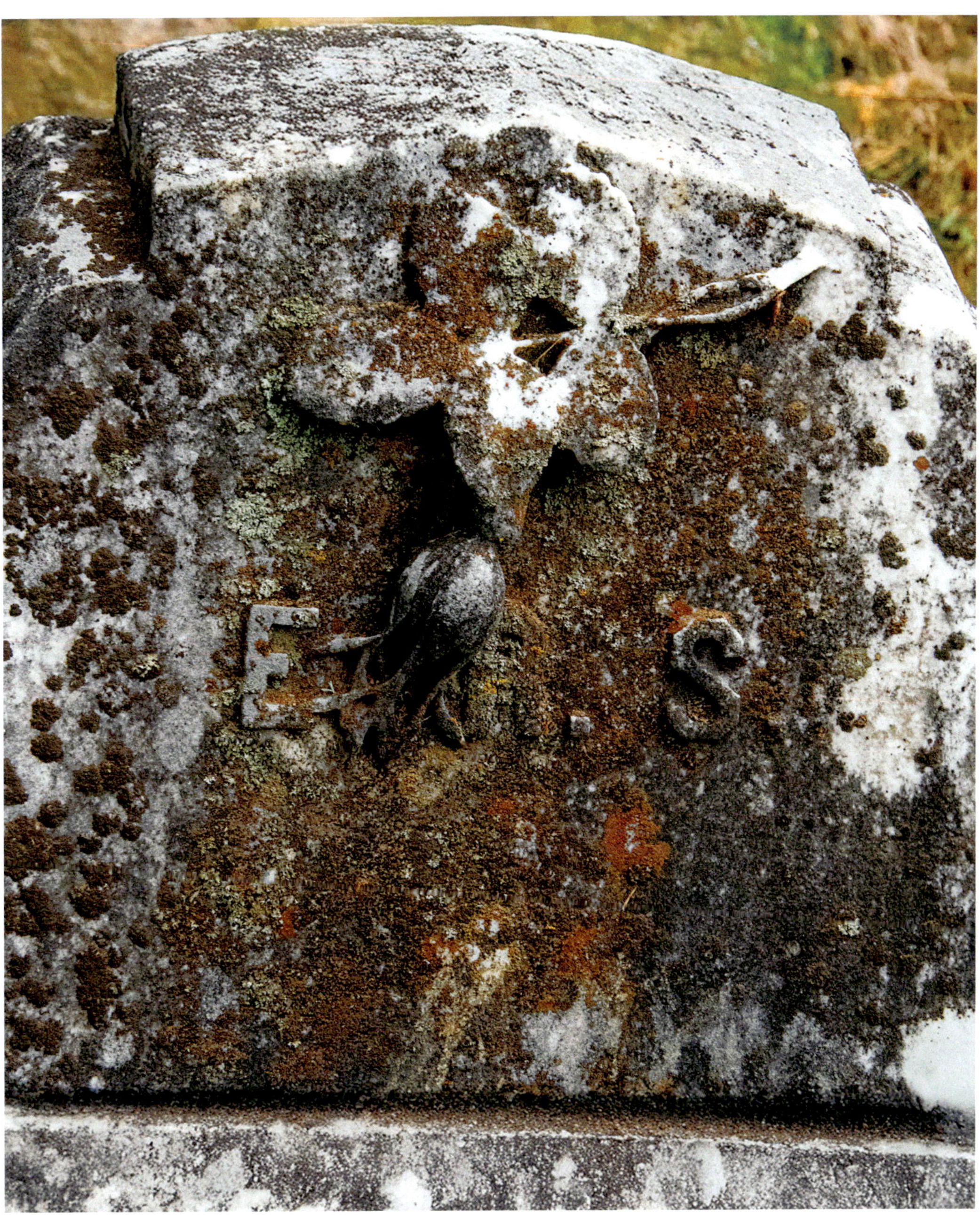

A rose bud on a grave marker means a life cut short in childhood. Hollins University Cemetery, Roanoke, Virginia.

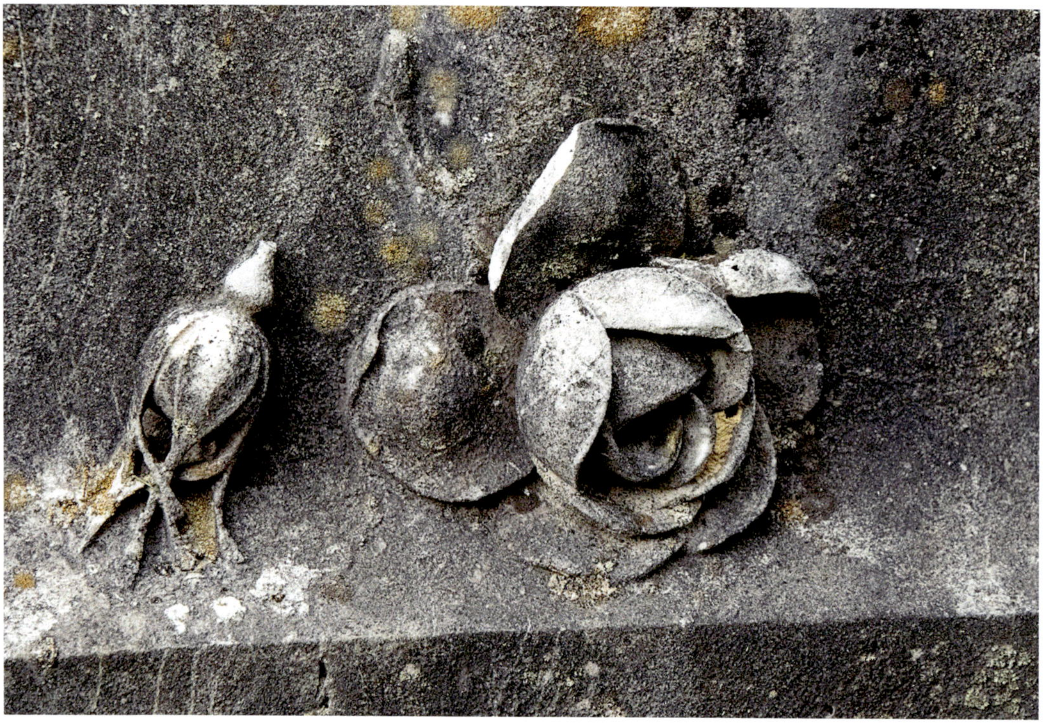

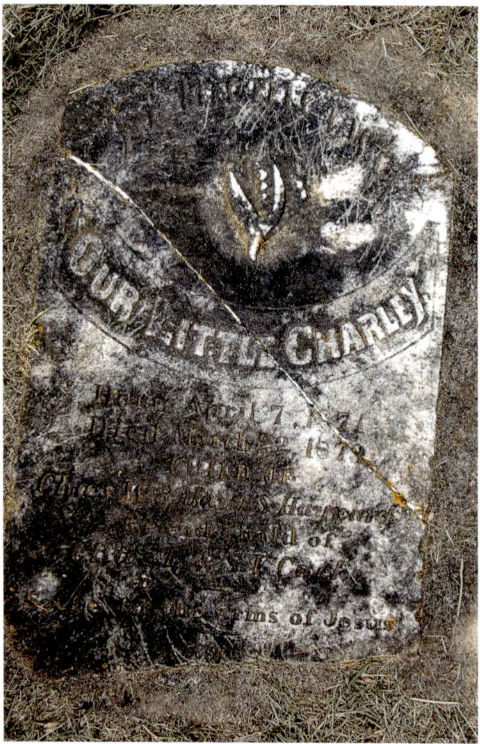

Above: A rose bud, and a partial open rose means a life cut short, usually teen or early twenties. Hollins University Cemetery, Roanoke, Virginia

Left: Little Charlie. The sweet pea on the stone indicates a child. Hollins University Cemetery, Roanoke, Virginia.

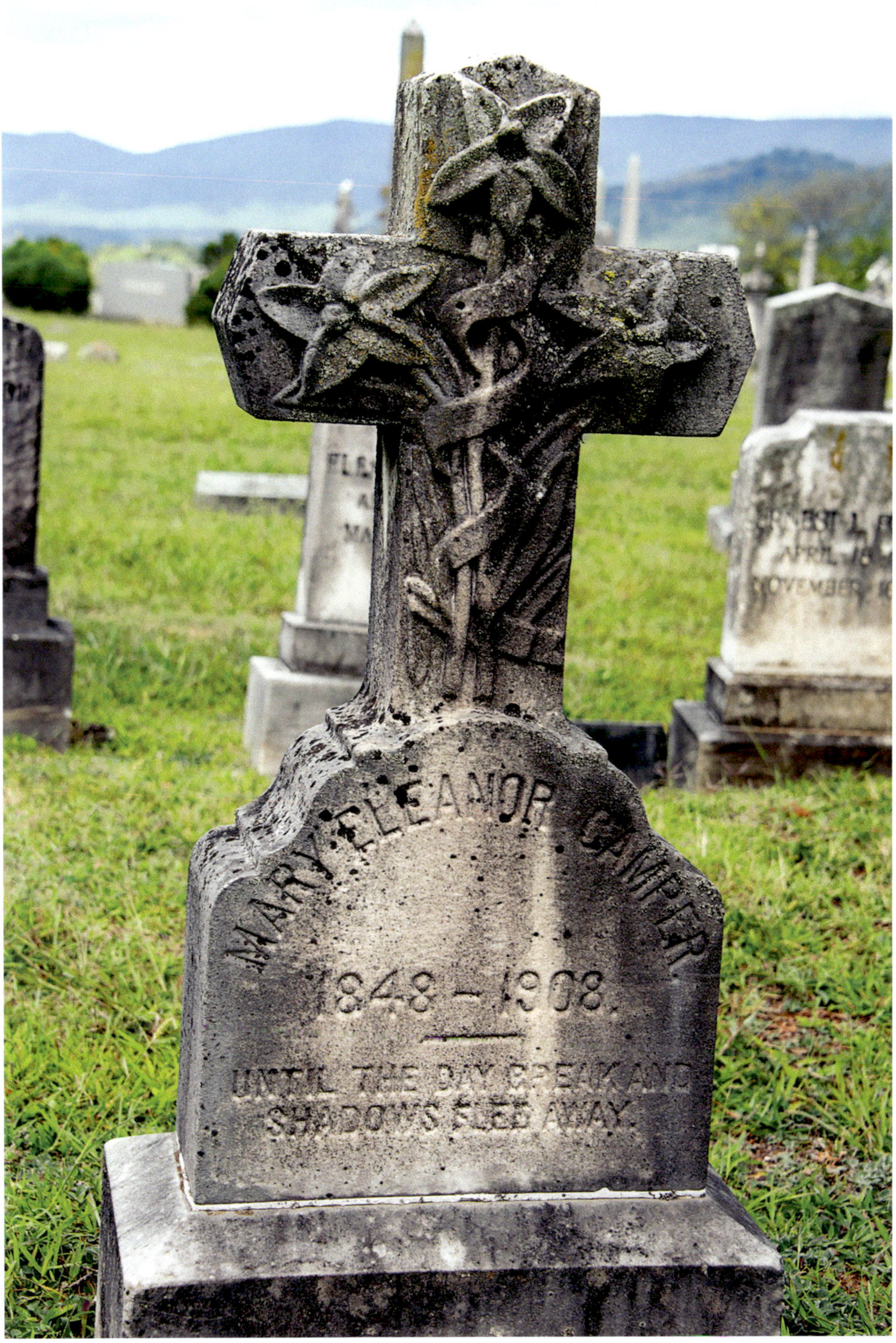

"Until the daybreak and shadows flee away." Epitaph on a stone with carved Easter lilies, symbolizing resurrection and innocence of the soul. Located in East Hill Cemetery.

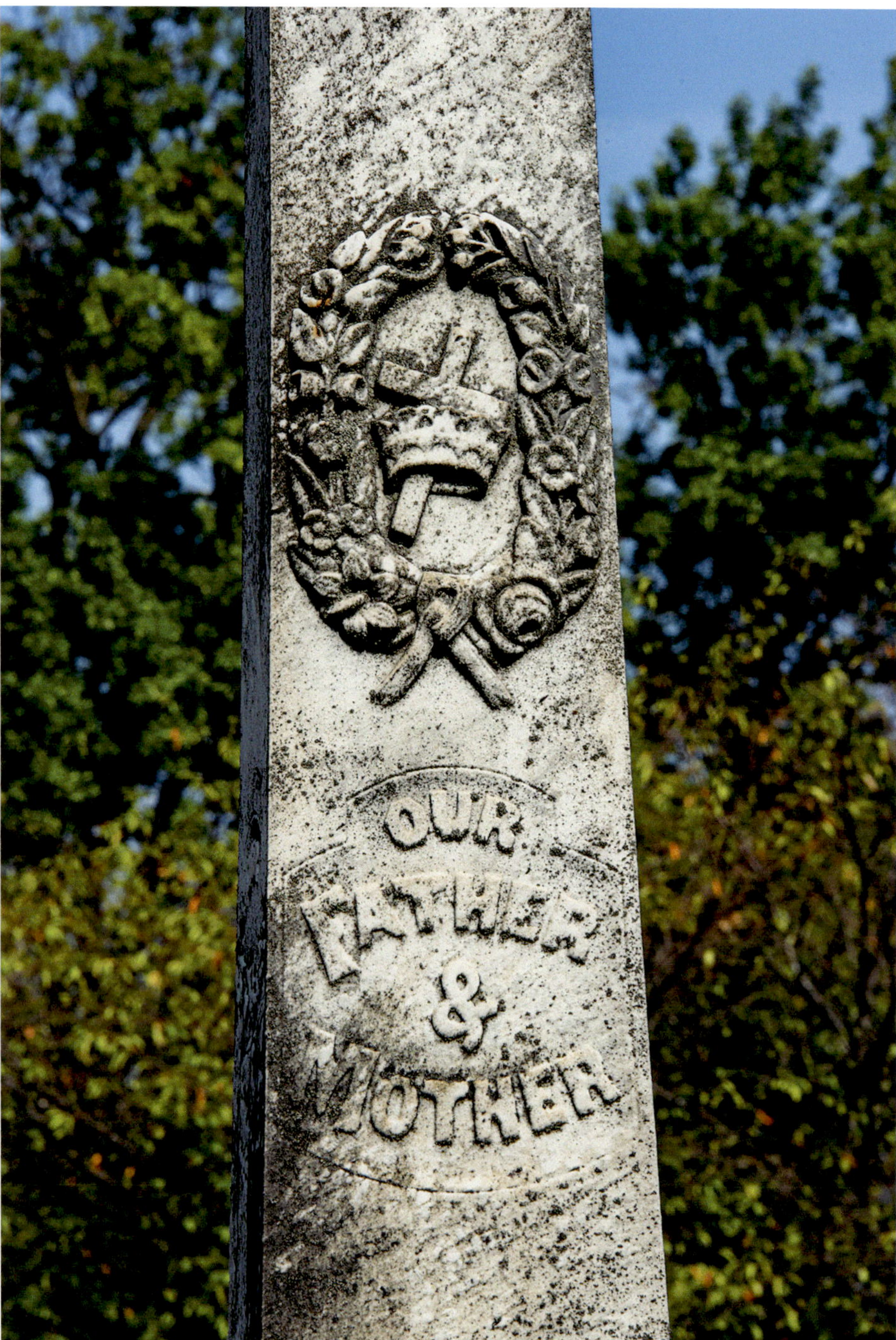

This stone is rich with symbolism. A wreath encompassing Easter lilies, resurrection and the innocence of the soul; Calla lilies, marriage and fidelity; morning glories, morality and farewell; a single rose in full bloom, a life fully lived; and the wreath, the intertwining of their lives. The cross and crown in the middle represent victory over death through Christ.

The old ways of the Appalachia region and, therefore, Southwest Virginia developed out of the melding of multiple cultures coming together and intermingling over the generations. So, it is not uncommon to find aspects from multiple cultures. Over time, this would develop into a set way of doing things, to include how deaths, mourning, and burials were conducted.

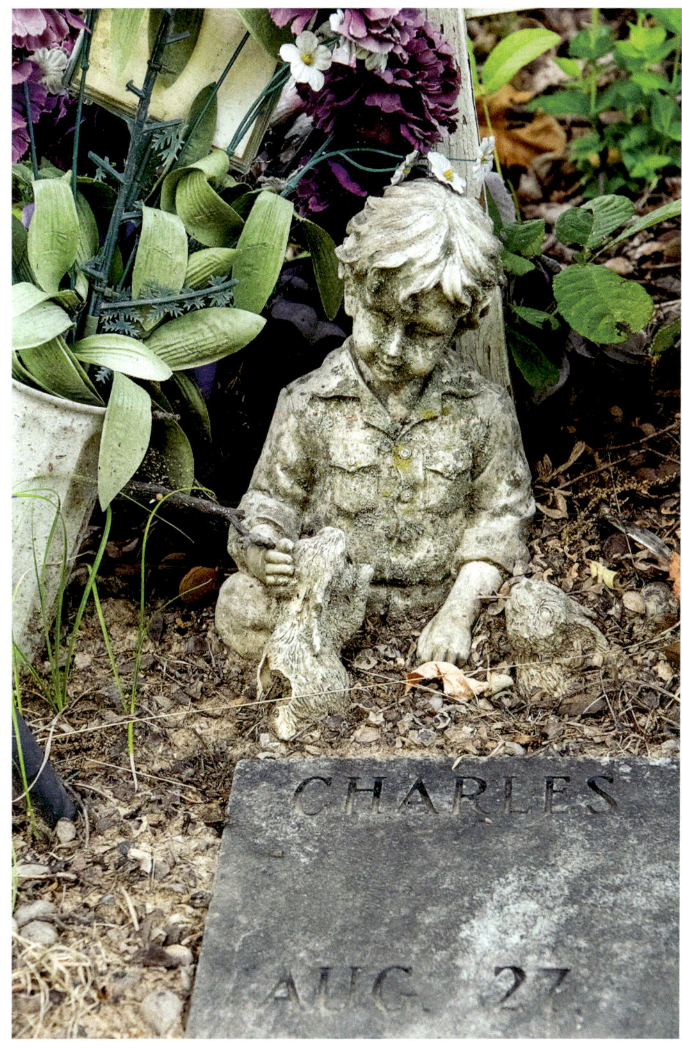

Personal items left on graves are very common even today in the region. Toys, small tokens, pennies (a penny for your thoughts) are placed to let the deceased know they are in your thoughts. Small statuary that is reminiscent of the loved one is particularly meaningful.

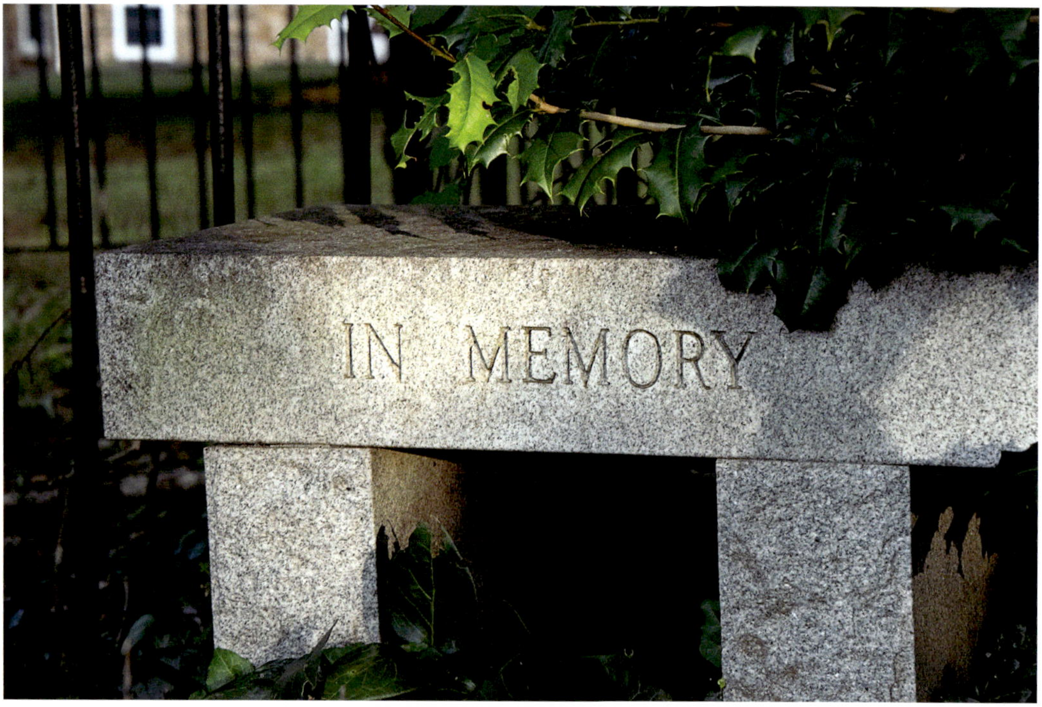

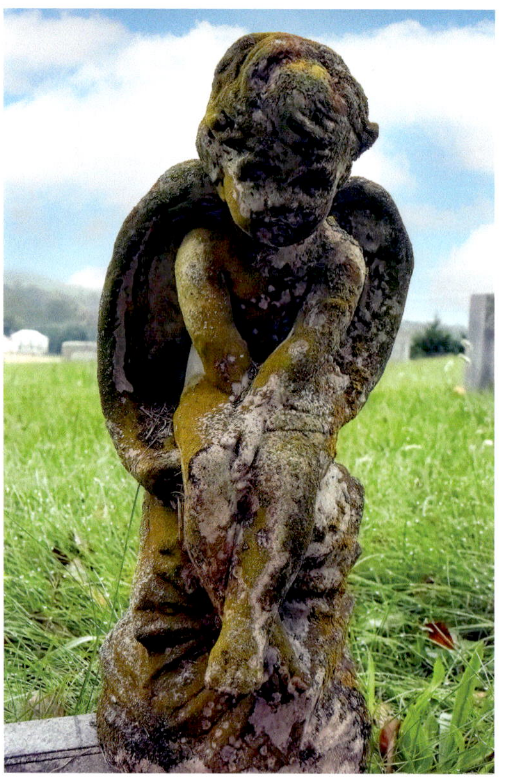

Above: Simple memorials of remembrance are popular in the cemeteries, encouraging those left behind to visit and embrace the memory of their loved ones in peace. Fincastle Presbyterian graveyard.

Left: In the mountain cemeteries, it is more common to place simple and personal items of remembrance. Locust Bottom Cemetery, Botetourt County.

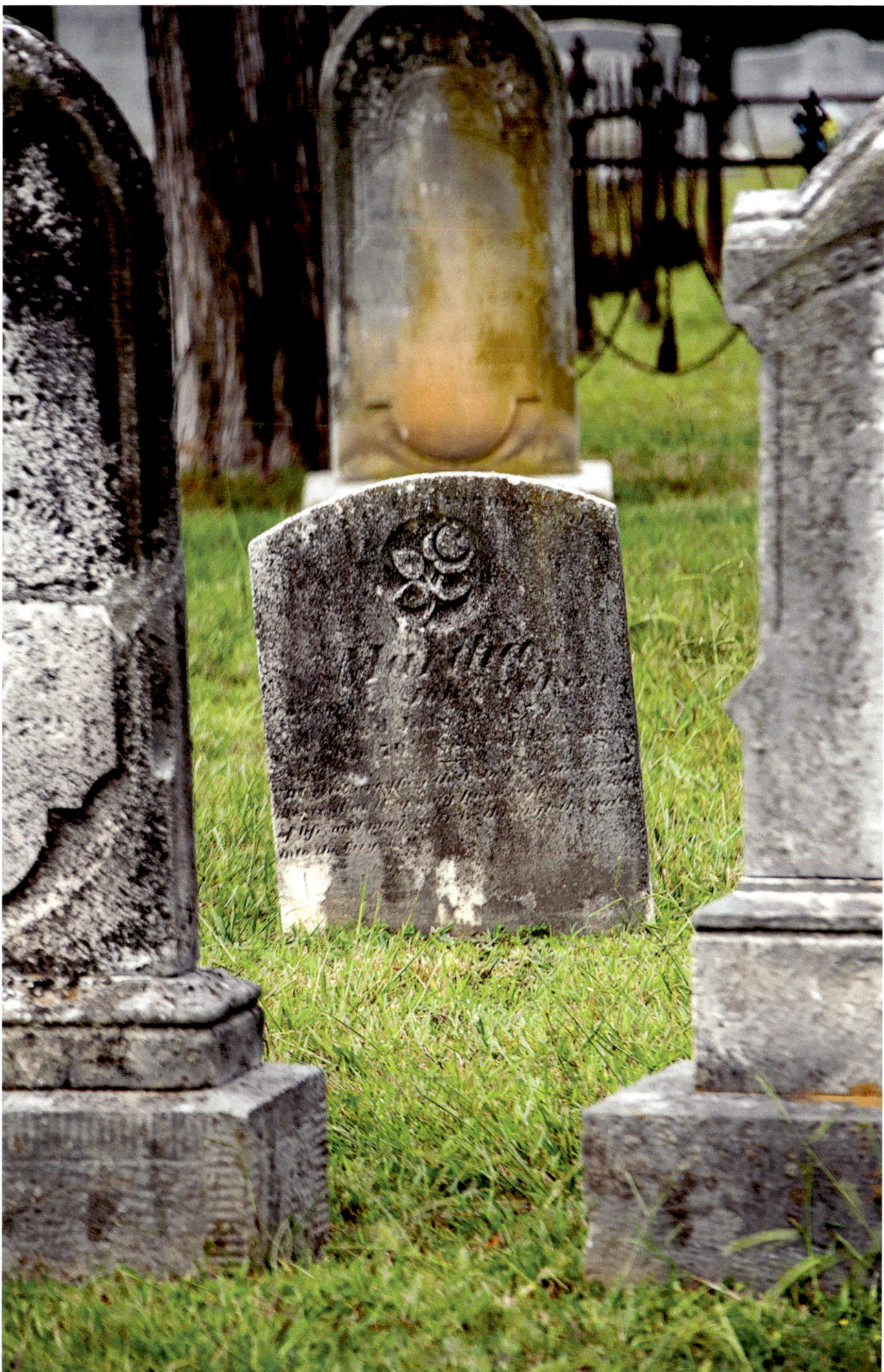

Martha. The rose fully bloomed indicates a full life. Located in East Hill Cemetery, Salem, Virginia.

During the early years of Southwest Virginia, in small areas the local church bell would toll to alert the community that a death had occurred. It would generally chime once for every year of age, helping to identify for whom it could be tolling. This helped to organize what needed to be done to assist the family and gather the community. Family and friends would stop what they were doing to proceed to the family that needed assistance. The men would gather to dig the grave and build the coffin.

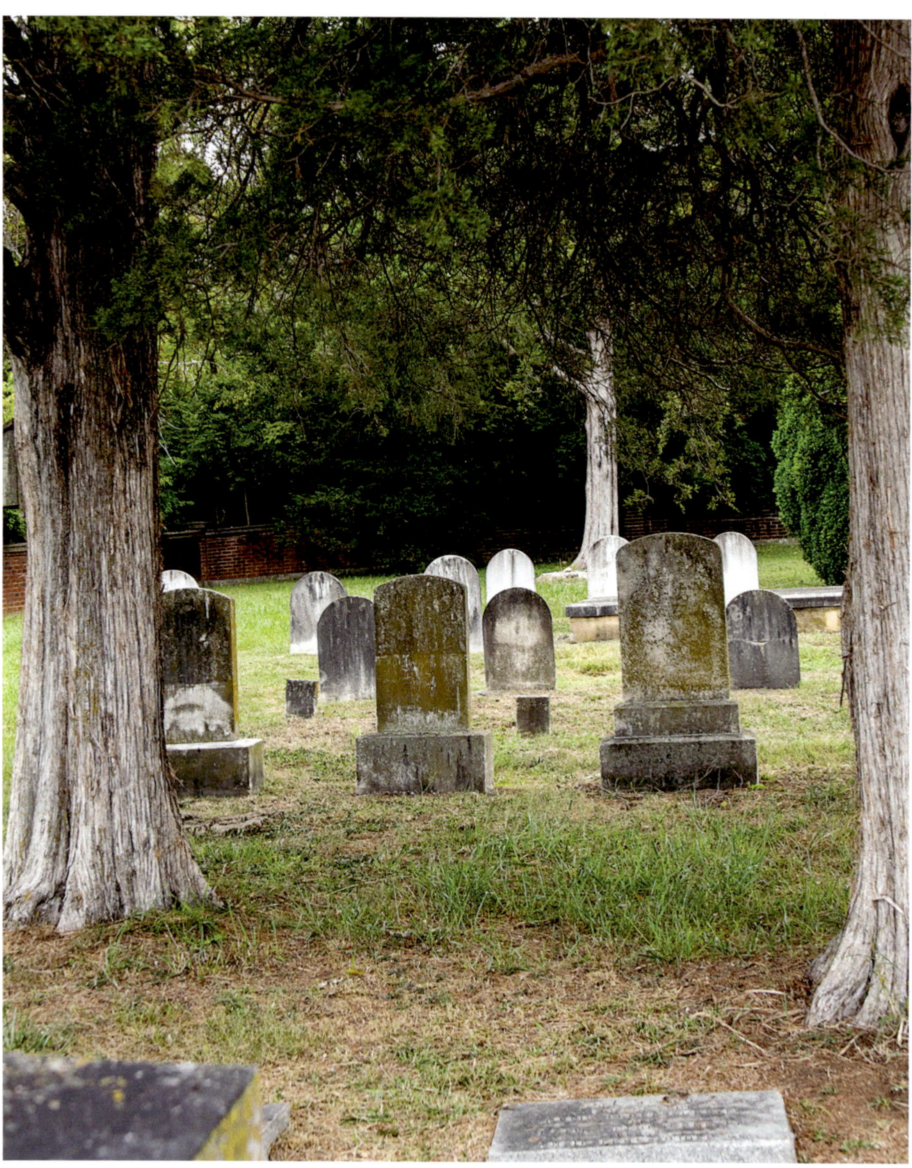

Small community cemeteries were more common in earlier days, and universities were their own communities with faculty and staff living in or around the schools. Hollins University Cemetery, Roanoke, Virginia.

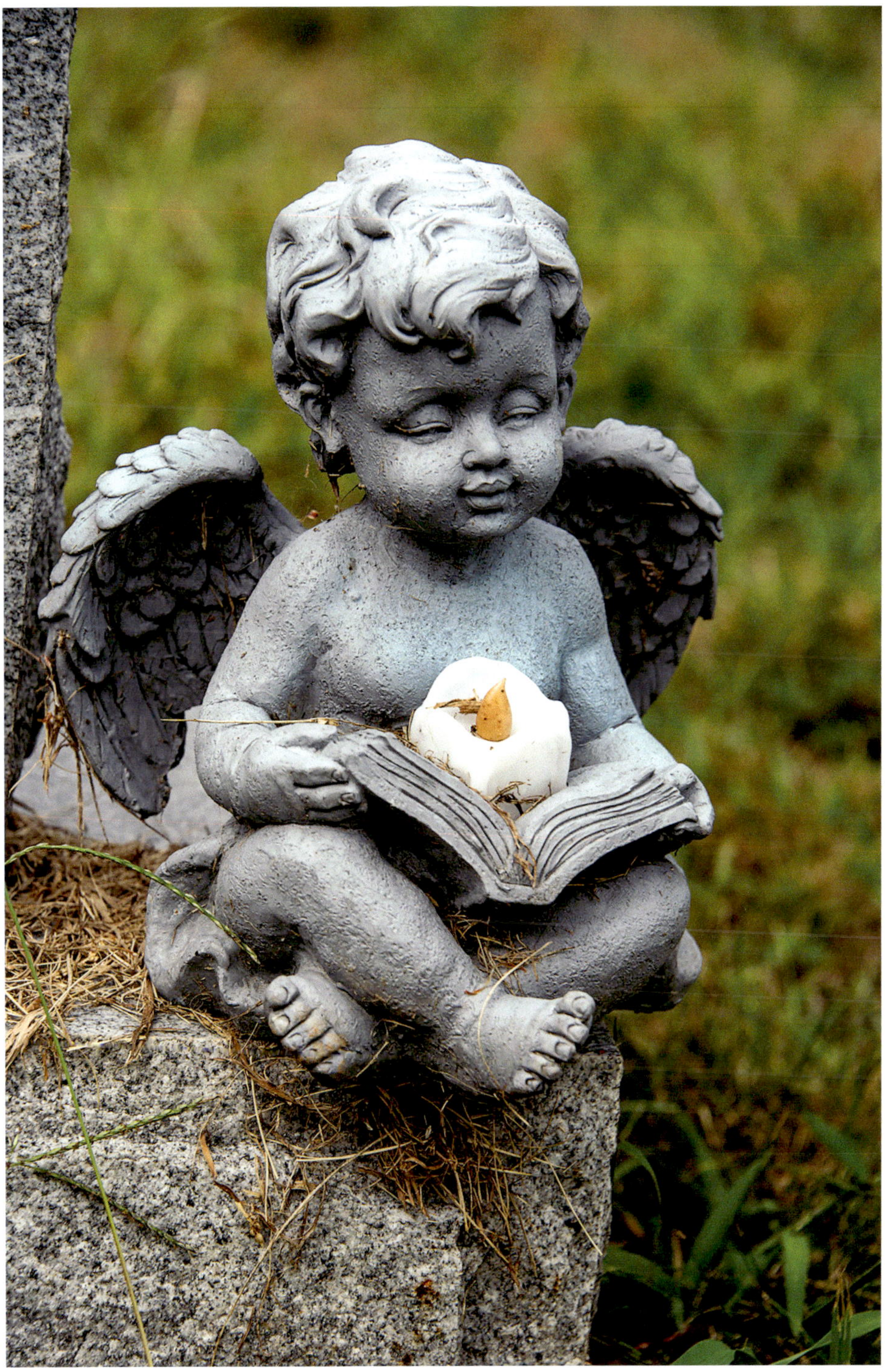

Personal tokens for the loved one imbued with light were hope for their soul to find the peace and light promised in death. Unnamed mountain cemetery.

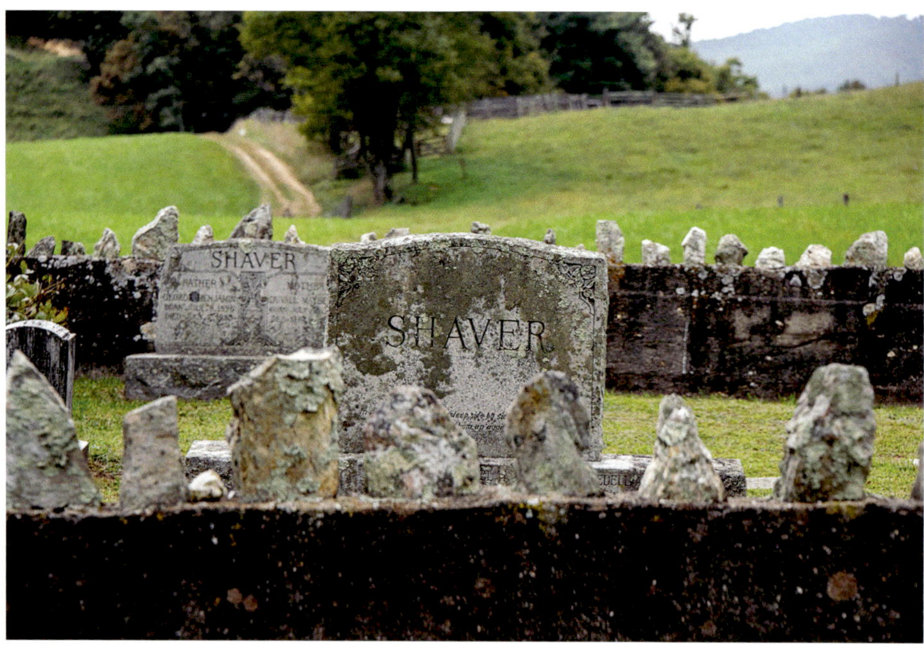

Shaver Cemetery, Blue Ridge Parkway. Old rock and mortar fence with local stone for decoration and to deter livestock and wildlife large enough to damage the stones. Some are basic field stone; others are field stone with white quartz in raw form.

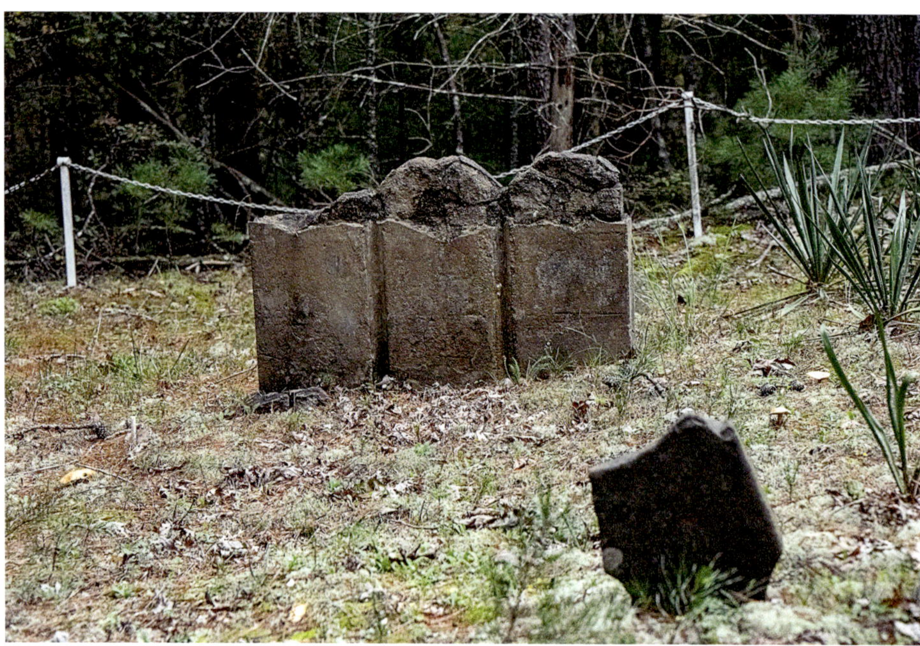

Unnamed mountain cemetery. Stones weathered by time and the descendants passed from living memory.

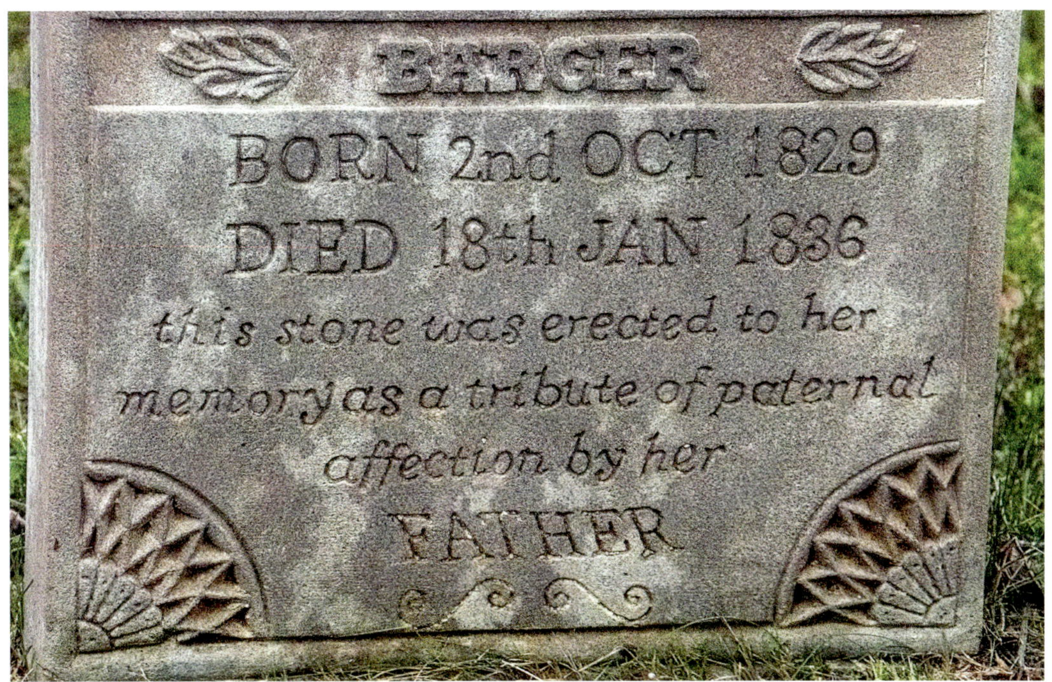

Above: Time taken by a father to lovingly remember his daughter. Barger Cemetery, Blacksburg, Virginia.

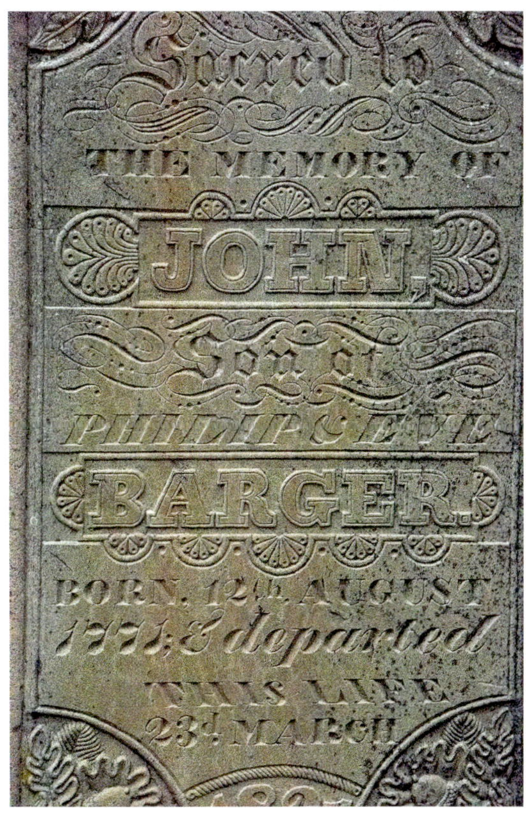

Right: Beautifully detailed stone carved with great care. Cemetery that was once a small private rural cemetery, now with a city grown up around it, adjacent to Virginia Tech facilities.

Once the bell tolled, every mirror in the house would be covered with cloth. This was to prevent the spirit getting distracted and getting "lost" in the glass. The hands of clocks were also stopped to record the time of death but also to start the mourning process. For the family, time would stand still until the last guest had gone home from the wake. The clocks would then be restarted, and life would move on.

The preparation of the body varied slightly depending on the root culture of the family. Scottish traditions would practice saining which was blessing and protecting the body. The oldest female in the family would light a candle and wave it over the body three times, three handfuls of salt were placed in a wooden bowl and put upon the chest.

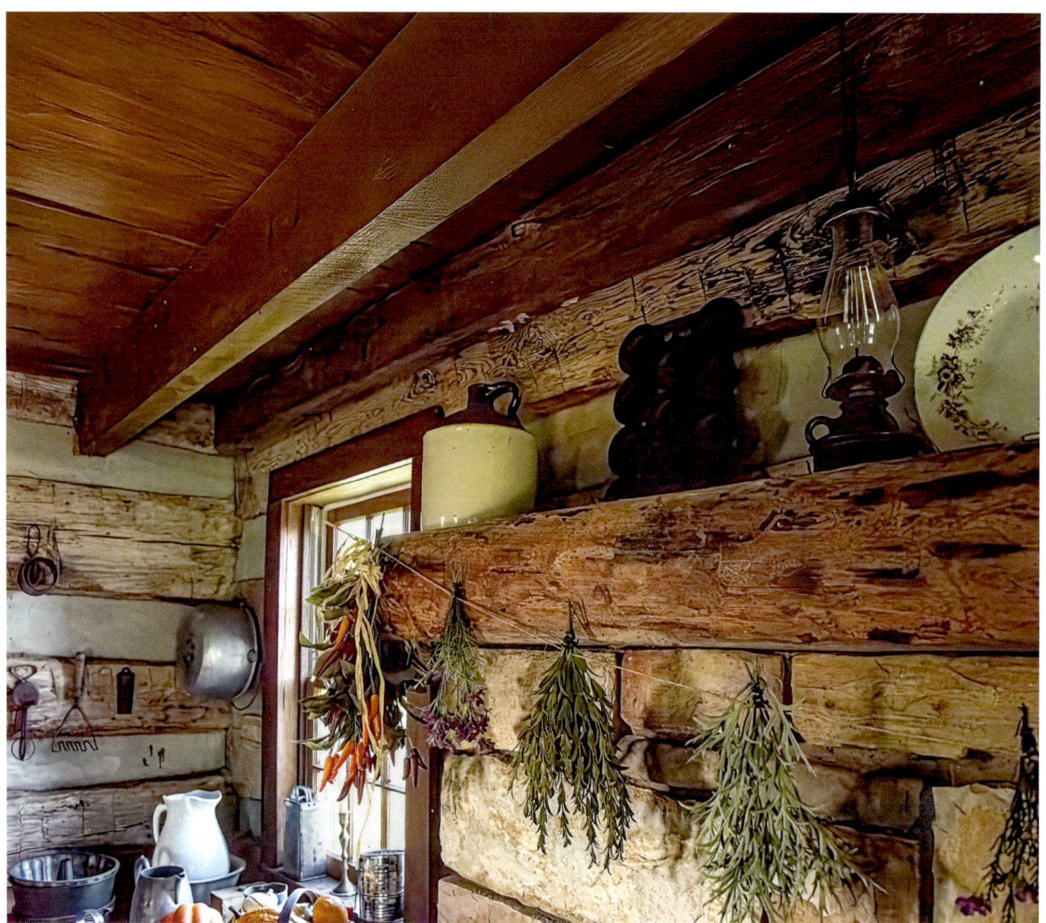

Herbs and flowers were used to keep the body fresh as sitting up with the dead, where we get the word "wake," was transpiring before the services and burial.

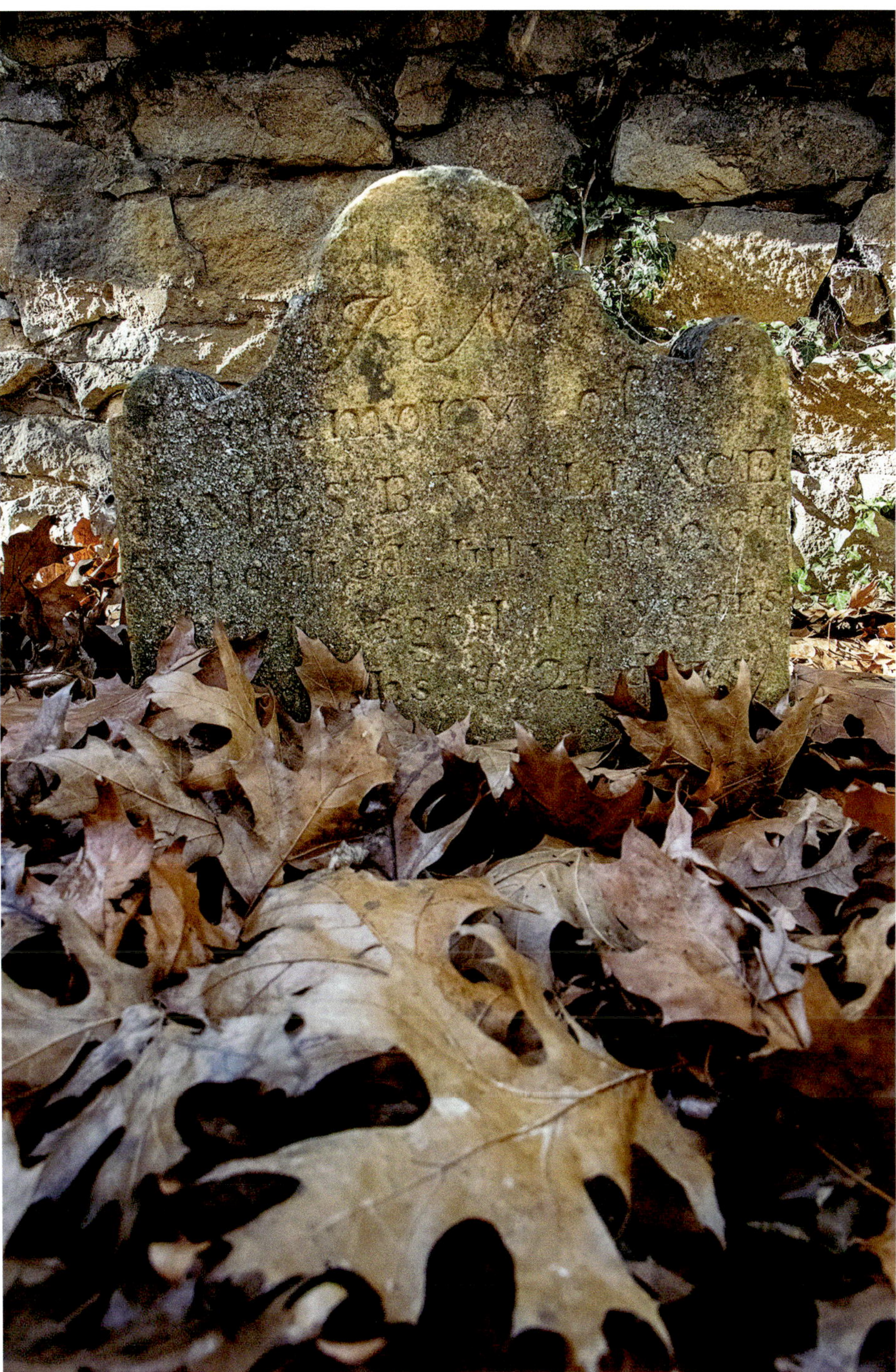

Early preparations were handled at home, the grave dug by friends and family. Stone from this era. "In Memory of James B Wallace," most likely Scottish. Oak Grove Cemetery, Lexington, Virginia.

The arms were folded across the chest, feet were brought together and tied there, coins made of silver, or fifty cent pieces were placed on the eyelids for weights to keep them closed and a cloth tied around the chin to keep the mouth shut. Copper coins were not used as the metal would turn the skin green. There were several methods to prevent discoloration of the skin until it was time for viewing. Aspirin in water or soda water were soaked in a towel and laid over the face. Washing with lye soap and a cloth dipped in camphor, vinegar, or alcohol over exposed skin were also methods. These were other reasons for the dead to not be left unattended as the cloth was not allowed to dry out.

Some cultural backgrounds also saw the coins as having other purposes. Some European cultures believed if the eyes were not shut, the dead would look for and take another person to accompany them on their journey. Others were held over from mythologies that stated the coins were payment for the ferryman of the underworld. Others thought they were a bribe to ensure safe passage.

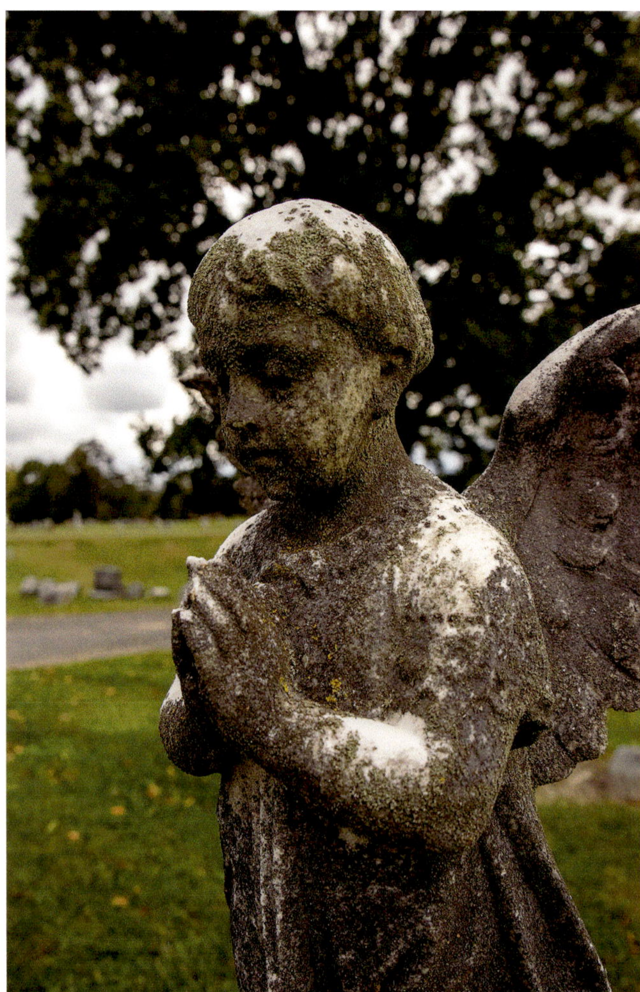

Statues were often created or brought by family, a time when the grave was more personalized. It usually represented the deceased child rather than a common icon representative of all boys or girls.

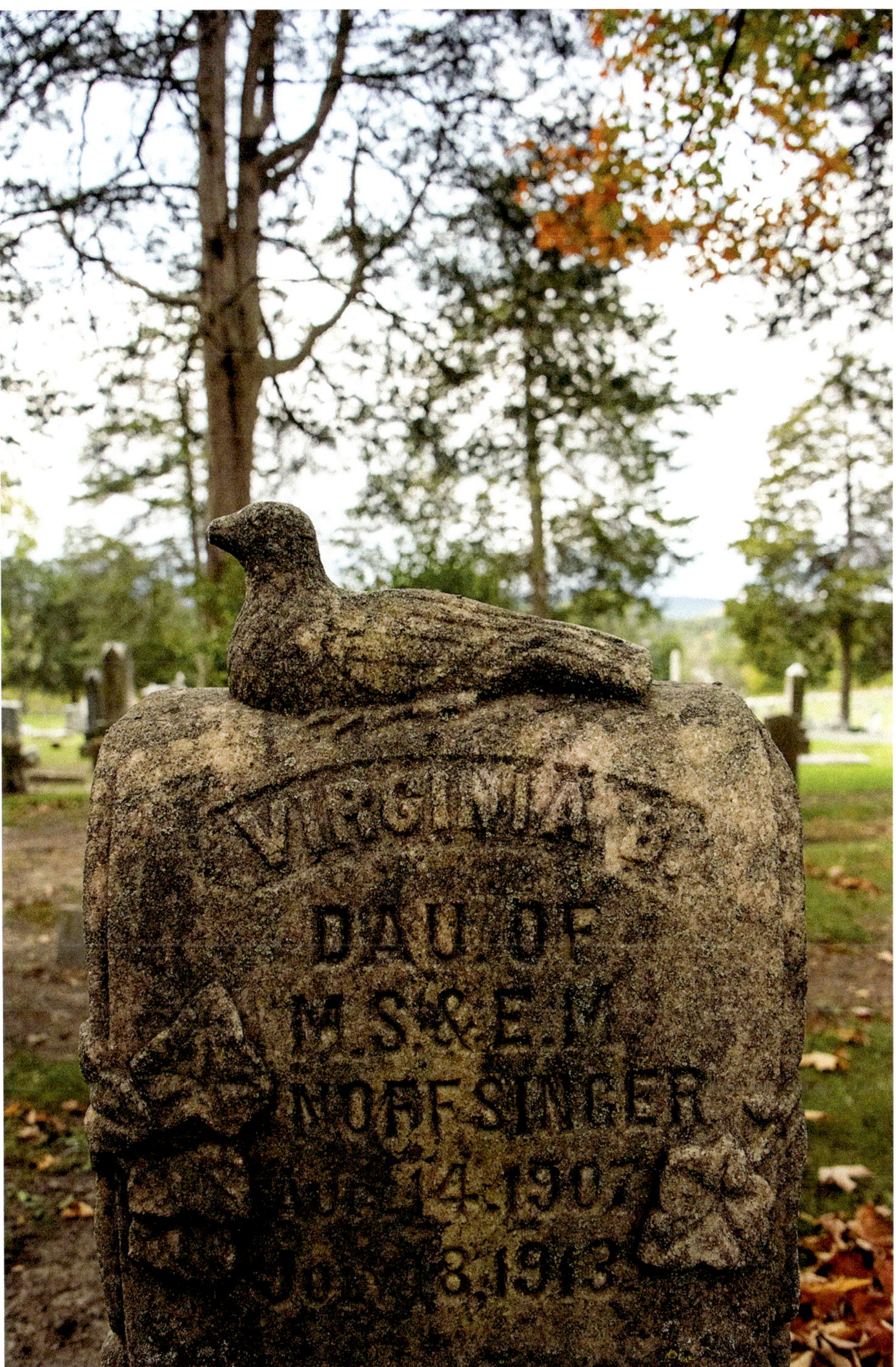

A dove on a tombstone was a symbol of innocence, so it was most often used for young children. Child mortality rates were high, and these stones were given great care and important symbolism.

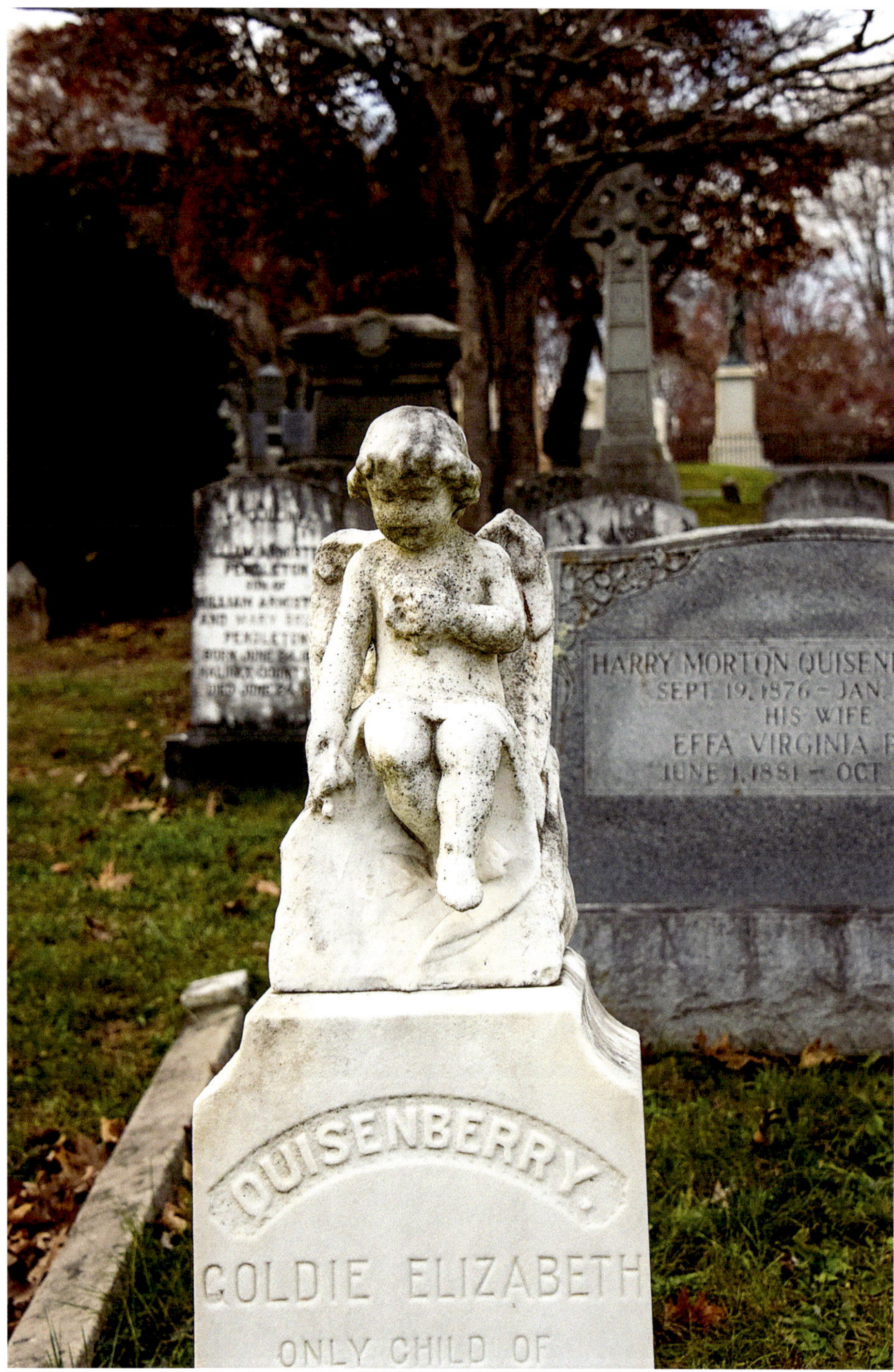

The loss of a child was more common, and statuary was often used to depict an eternal image of the lost child. White stones were particularly uncommon and when they were used it was often for special graves, like this one of an only child.

Original coffins were made from large tree trunks and so were called "tree coffins." As these were work intensive, pine boxes eventually replaced them as the mills that cut the boards became more commonplace. If the ground was frozen, then digging would have to wait until spring and the deceased would be stored somewhere cold until the ground thawed. It is important to note that the climate has changed considerably since that time. The cold set in from mid-October or earlier and was not gone until mid-April to late spring.

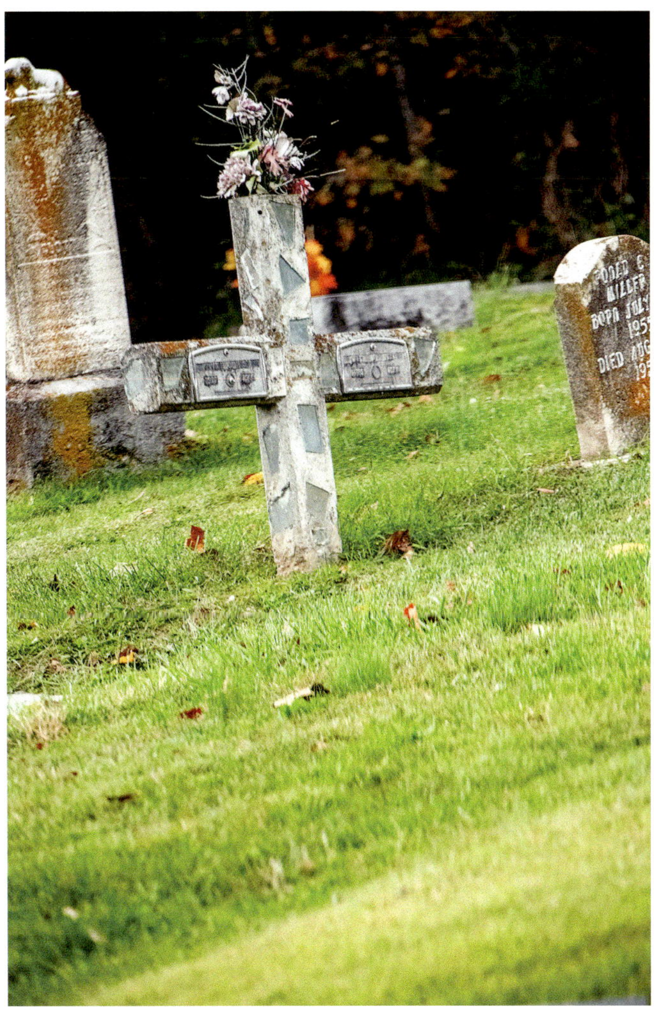

Grave markers were often done by the family out of available materials.

Superstition played a major role in many of these customs. One custom in particular that preceded the burial was known as sitting up with the dead. While it is rarely practiced today, this vigil for the dead was to keep watch over the deceased person's body. This became known as a "wake" because those who stayed around the clock had to be awake and aware during their vigil.

There were multiple reasons for sitting up with the dead. Some were practical. Predation in a mountain range that houses scavengers of all shapes and sizes from racoons to bobcats to bears. Then there were the common rodents and insects to keep away from the body.

Another reason was ritual and inclusion. Sitting up with the dead was an honor whereby each person who participated had one last chance to complete an important task for the deceased or the family. It also gave them an opportunity to seek closure and to say anything they felt might need saying, as it was believed that the soul did not leave until the body was interred. A lack of internment created stories of gruesome hauntings; thus, it was important to locate and bury the dead as soon as possible in the case of unnatural deaths or disappearances. This superstition was often leveled against the Appalachian folk as an effective form of psychological warfare by enemies.

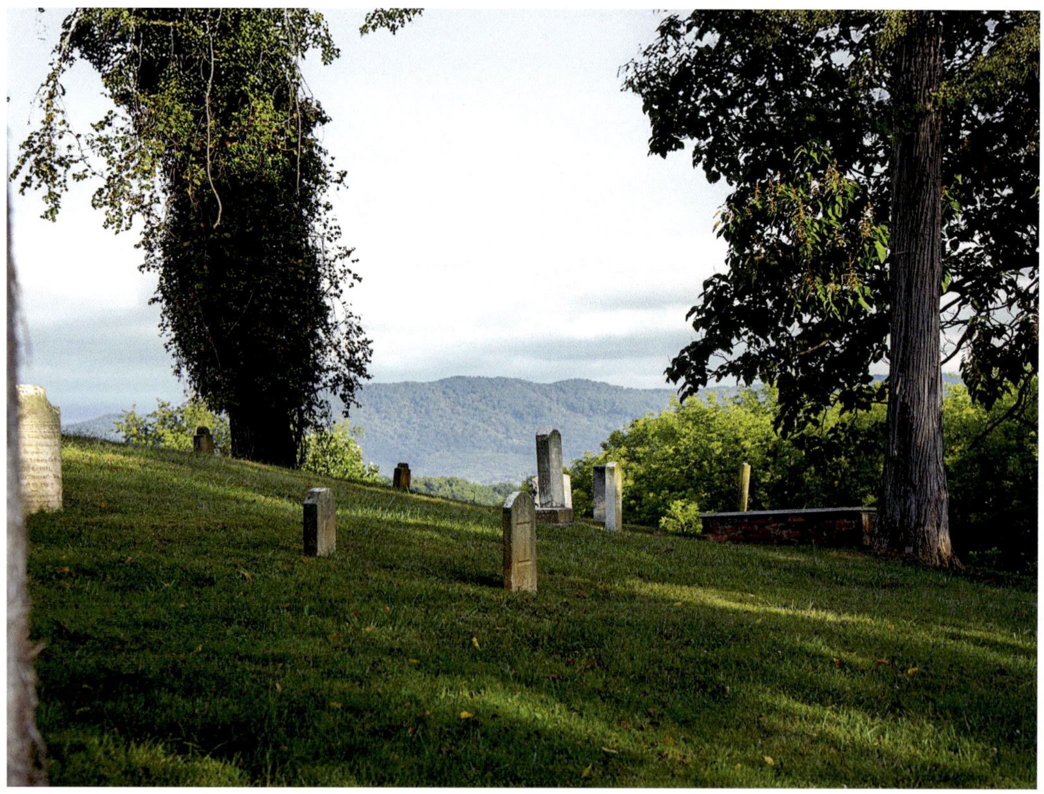

Small mountain communities would come together to bury community members in church yards. These graveyards served as places to socialize after church during the era of memorial gardens where it was common to picnic by your loved one's graves.

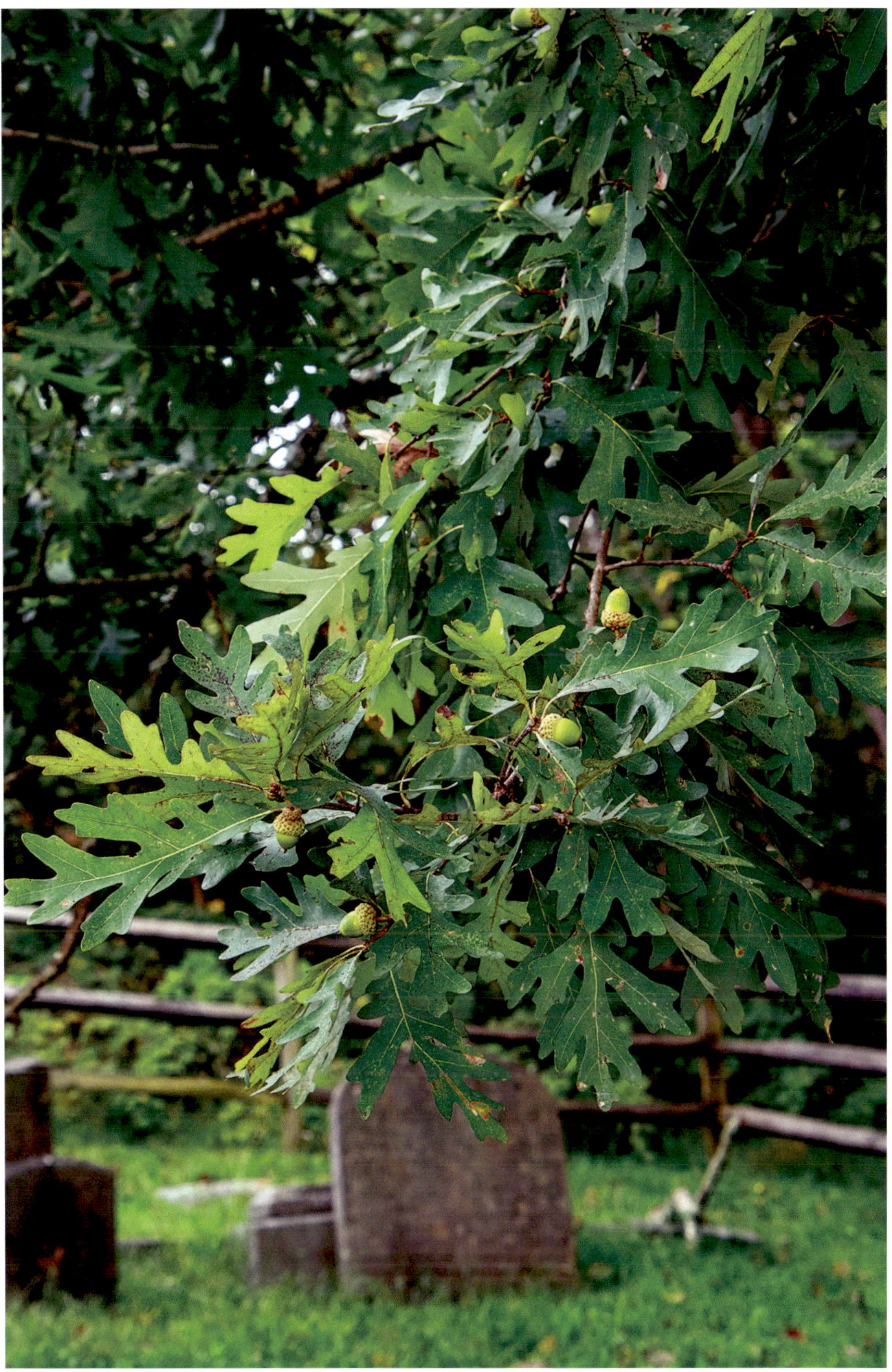

Oak trees were often planted on the boundaries of cemeteries for protection and as a representation of the strength of the family.

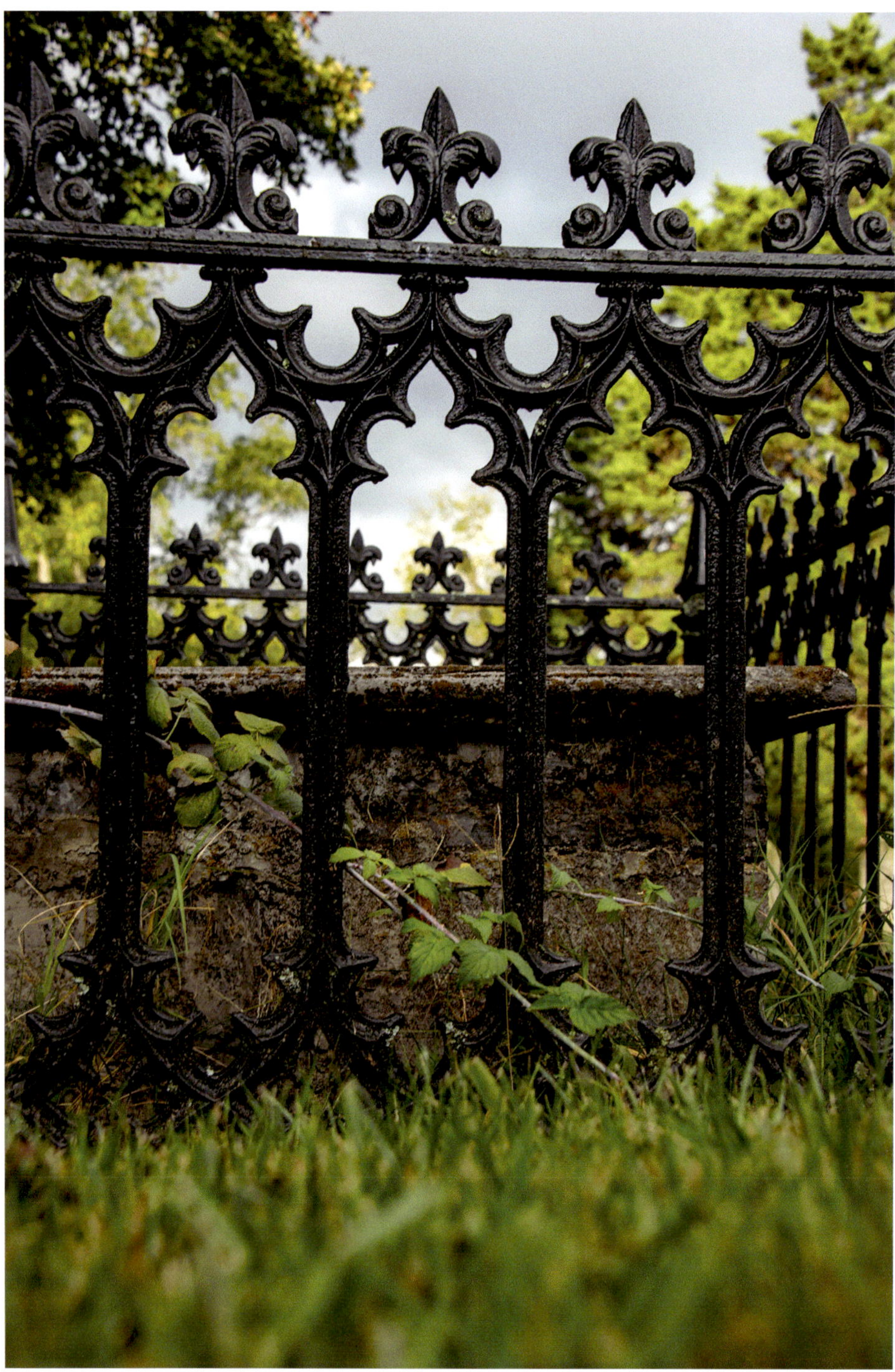

The crypt would be built of the materials at hand if the ground was too hard or rocky to dig graves as was often the case before tools for that specific task were readily available. The ornate fencing would have been added later to protect the crypt as it aged.

In some of the more extreme belief systems, sitting up with the dead was also intended to guard the body from spiritual appropriation. Some of the more antiquated beliefs that had made its way into Appalachia felt that the body was in danger of invasion by evil spirits between the time of death and the time of burial. Therefore, it was important that it not be left unattended and was also guarded by religious relics appropriate to their beliefs.

Sitting up with the dead also gave an opportunity for community and social interaction as it was a time to share stories and memories of the deceased.

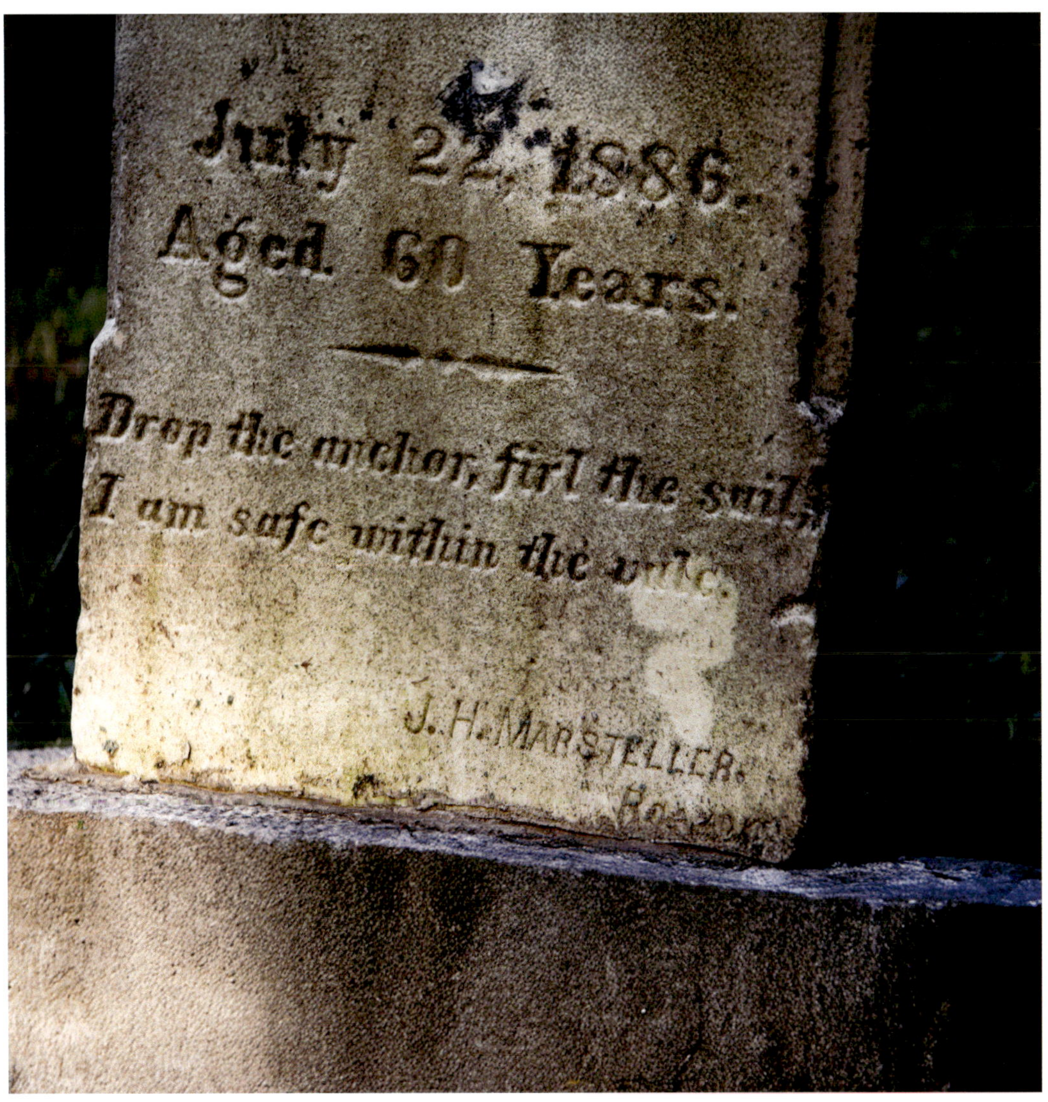

Epitaphs were often personalized when carving was available for a loved one. "Drop the anchor, firl the sail, I am safe within the vale." This one is from a hymn called Let Go the Anchor, which was popular at the time of internment (late 1800s).

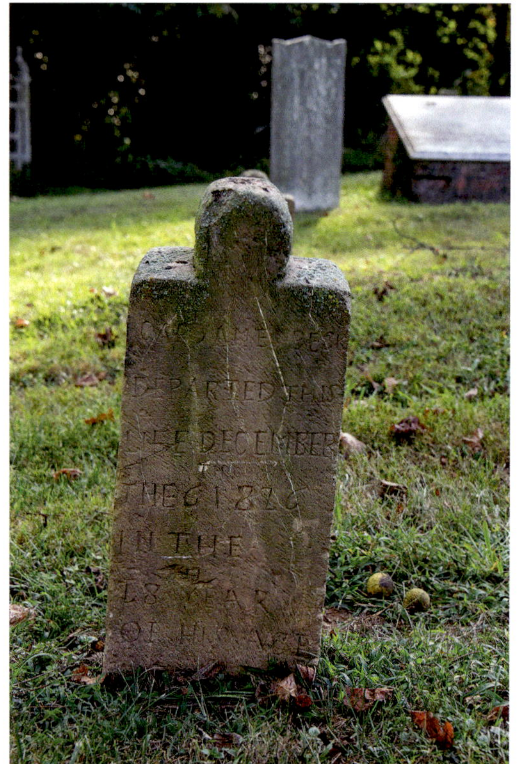

Left: Stones made of what was at hand (in this case baked clay, which is what bricks of the time were made of) and carved by the family are not uncommon in the oldest grave sites.

Below: Often because materials used were what was at hand—wood, or even early mortar—there are large areas of old cemeteries and graveyards that appear to be empty. Despite a lack of markers, they are completely filled. Their occupants pass out of living memory. There is no one to replace degraded or missing markers.

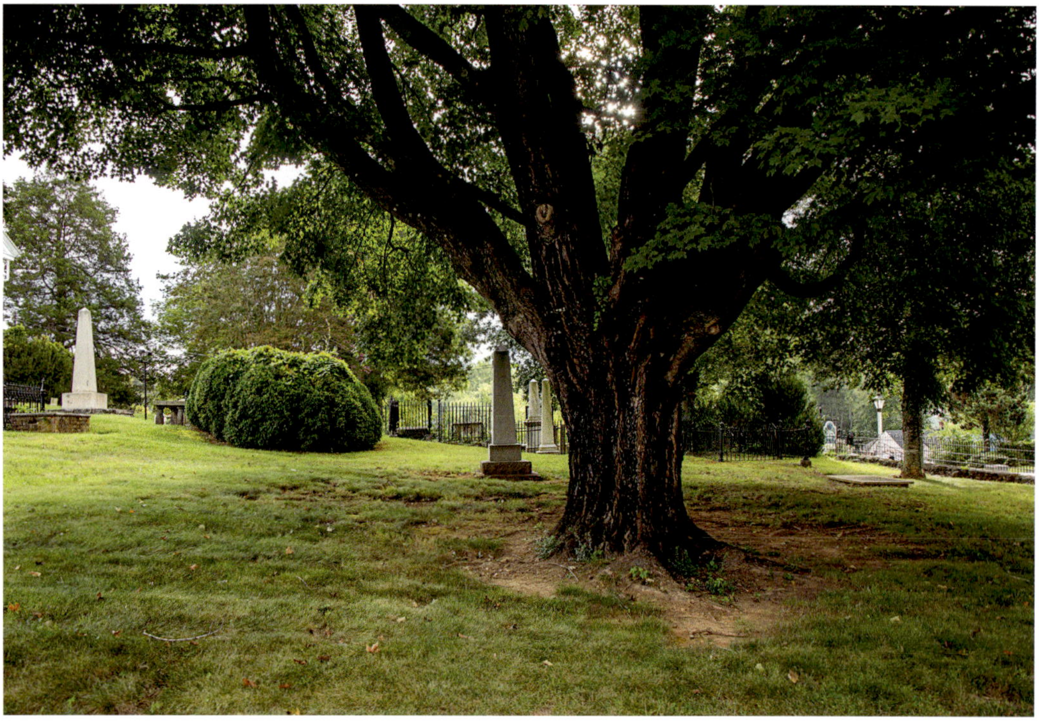

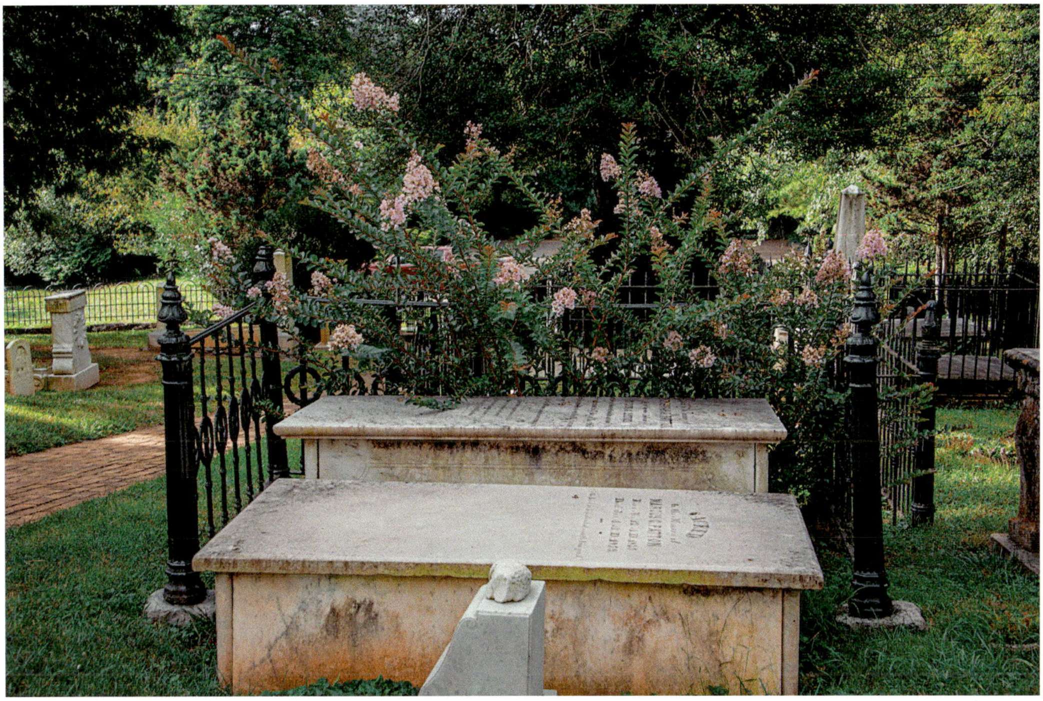

Above: It was not uncommon to plant a shrub, flower, or even a tree by a grave marker. The plant lives on even when markers fade away. Often cemeteries house heirloom plants that are uncommon to find in today's nurseries or greenhouses.

Right: Shrubs planted to ensure a site was marked or for aesthetic reasons will often overtake gravestones. In a twist, they will also often act to protect the stones from wear.

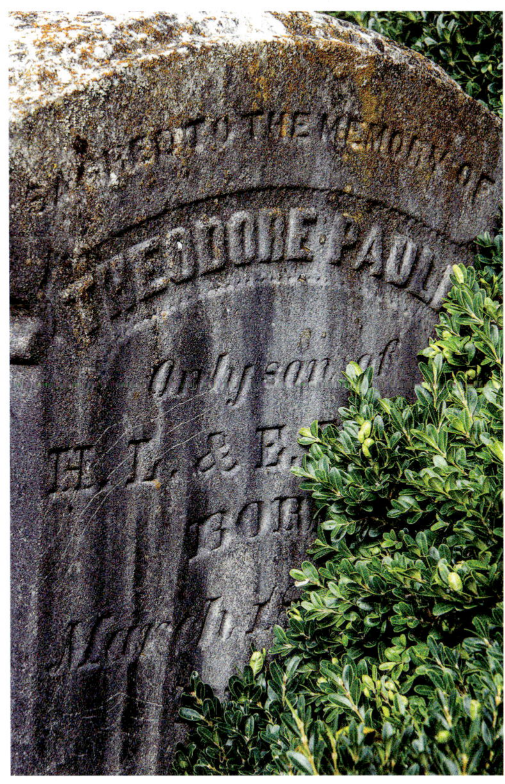

Flowers and herbs became part of the ritual of death to cover the odor of the decay that was taking place. Burials were generally performed within two days of death as preservation methods had not come into existence.

Sitting up with the dead started the night after death once the body was prepared and displayed. There was food and coffee, or tea made available to those sitting and a large breakfast was served. There would be another large meal right after the burial took place served by the community members. Today it is commonplace still to have the meal after the funeral with all the attendants contributing a prepared dish.

The superstitions of death intertwined with the everyday in Appalachia. Death was ever present due to accidents, illnesses, infant and mother mortality rates, among other causes. It left no room for argument. So, death was given a seat in the everyday with reverence. In larger houses, there were often two front doors, one to welcome company and the other a "funeral door," which led to a chamber where the departed were laid out and sitting up with the dead and other respectful visitation was honored.

At this time funeral homes and public cemeteries were unknown in these regions. Homes and communities were often spread out over several day's journey. Caring for the dead at home was necessary. The coffin was homemade, the deceased cleaned and dressed by family members and then laid out in this chamber. In the case of households where such opulent space was not reasonable, the family gathering room or a parlor would do.

The day after the wake, if there was a church near enough, the body would be loaded onto a wagon and taken for service. If there was not a church nearby there was a family plot specific to this purpose. It is not uncommon to find small cemeteries very near old homes throughout Southwest Virginia.

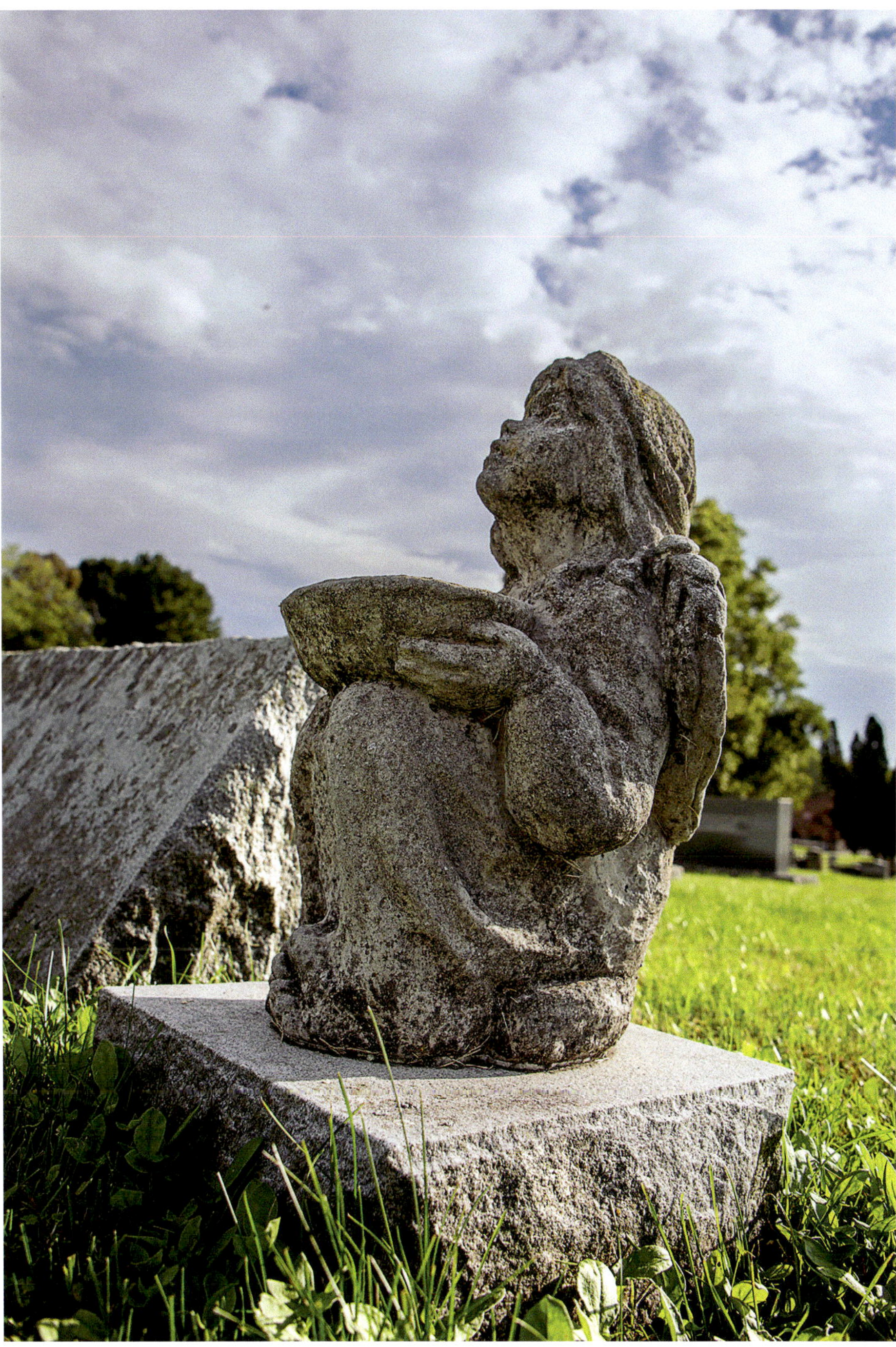

Representations of loved ones or small statuary they might have liked are often installed at the graves. This one seems to be waiting; the bowl likely once held a potted flower or acted as a small wishing well. Wishing wells are not uncommon in the regions cemeteries. It was thought that the well wishes or thoughts left in the well made their way to the loved ones.

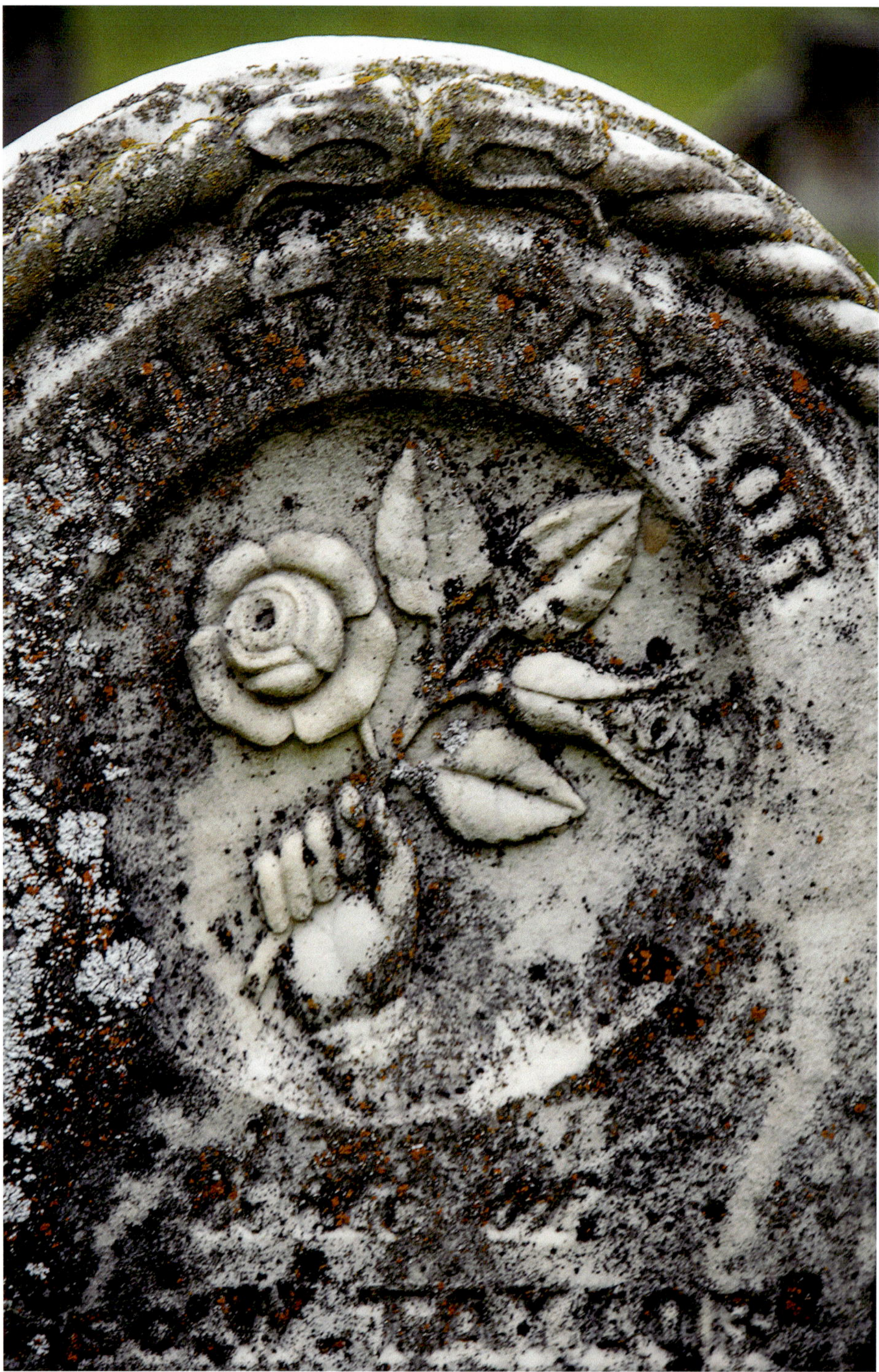

A rose in full bloom for a full life but held by the stem represents the thorns experienced in the process and the bitterness of the loss.

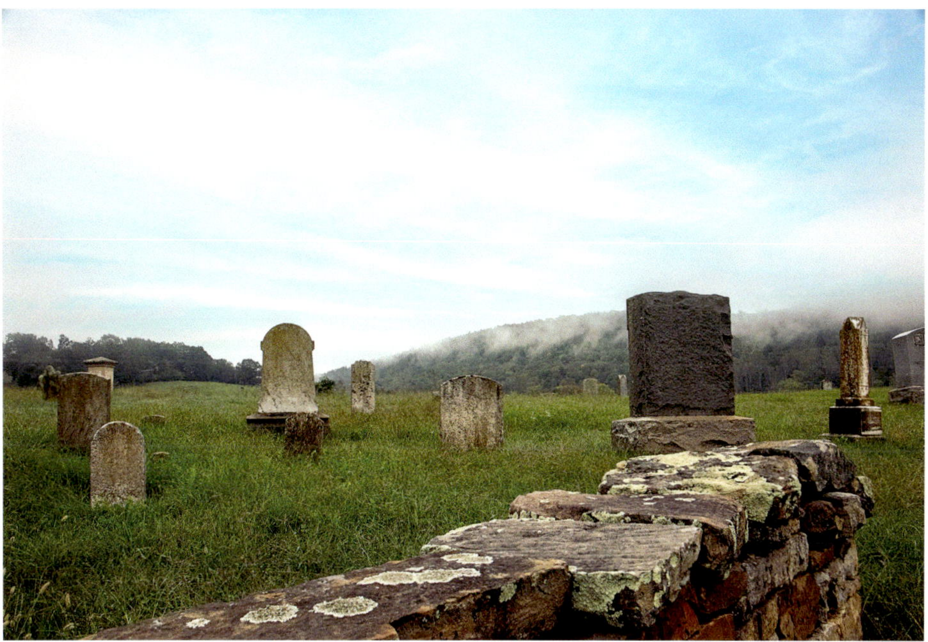

A mountain cemetery where the community would gather to lay loved ones to rest after services.

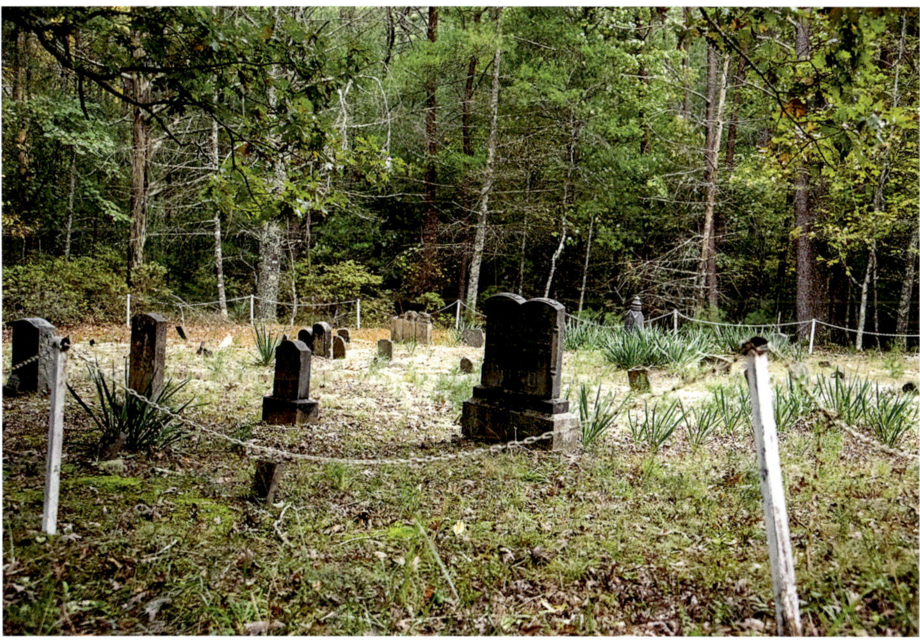

Mountain cemeteries were often closer than anything else to the homes. After a service at home, loved ones would be laid to rest in the peace of the mountains. Yucca were common plants for graves as they were hardy and bloomed once a year without spreading quickly or growing very large. They also were symbols of protection, loyalty, and purity.

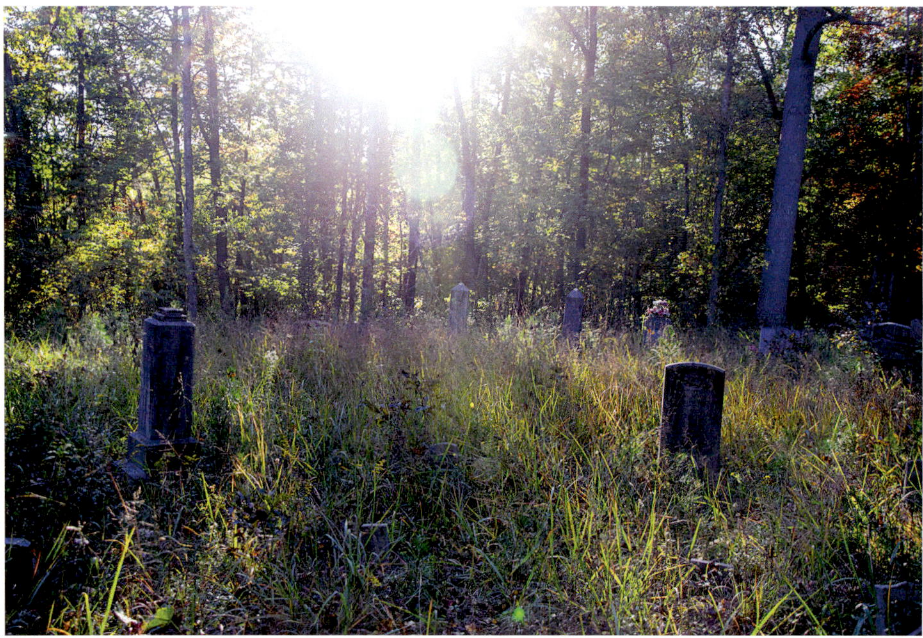

Rural cemeteries deep in the forest were common places of internment for the peaceful surroundings.

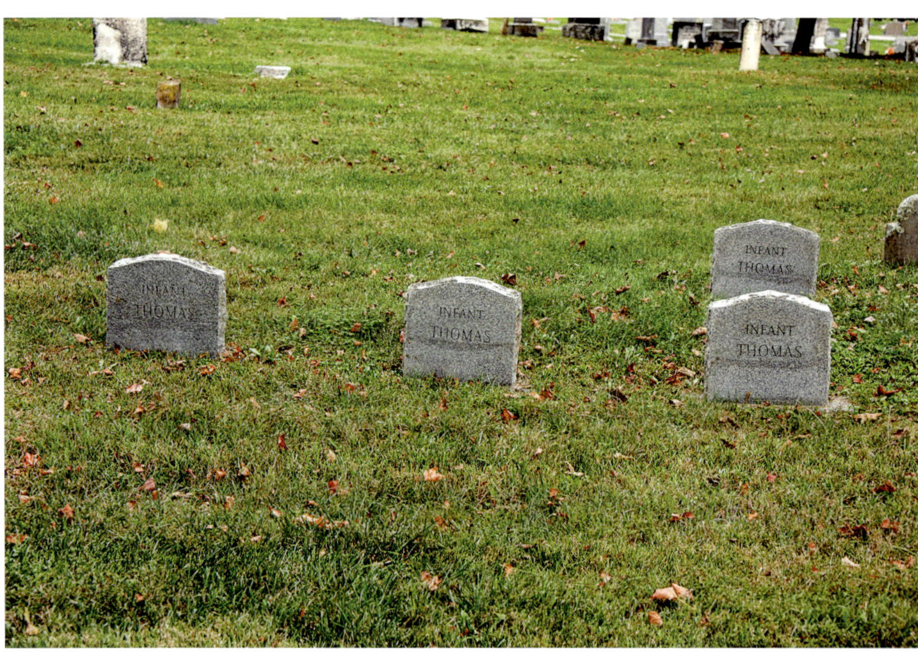

Childbearing and birth were very difficult matters. Many children did not survive. It is not unusual for family plots to have many infant stones, especially during periods of epidemic such as that of 1918.

Following behind the wagon were the family. The bell would toll until the casket was brought inside, where the last viewing for friends and family took place. At that time, some would place objects into the coffin that either meant something to them or they felt would mean something to the deceased. Once the coffin was closed, there would be a procession on foot behind the wagon to the burial or through the church yard if there was a graveyard on hand.

One important aspect of the burial itself was the laying of the body and filling in of the grave. It was commonplace for the direct family to be left to the task of completing the burial. The phrase "we take care of our own" is commonly used throughout Appalachia, and this final act is a completing of that task for the person who has passed. While the family was completing this often-difficult task the rest of the community would prepare for the meal after burial by assisting with preparations at the family home. The last act of dedication to their loved one was, and even today is sometimes still, a sacred act.

A strong sense of community involvement created bonds that in these harsh environments were important to survival. They created social ties in times of hardship and sadness that allowed reciprocation when the tides were turned on other families. These same bonds would strengthen communities to band together in times of war as well. When the men would leave to fight in conflicts the community would band together to keep everyone's needs met.

The honor with which the graves of those who fell in these battles are kept, even centuries after their burials, are a testament. An undying dedication to independence and freedom that were and are still venerated.

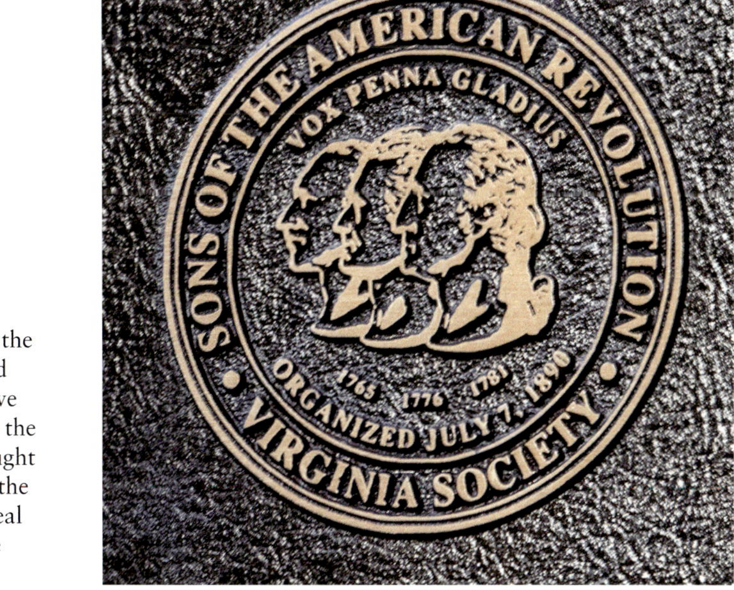

Patriotism runs deep in the Appalachian region, and groups exist to keep alive the history and care for the graves of those who fought for our nation. Sons of the American Revolution Seal is found throughout the late 1800s up to today.

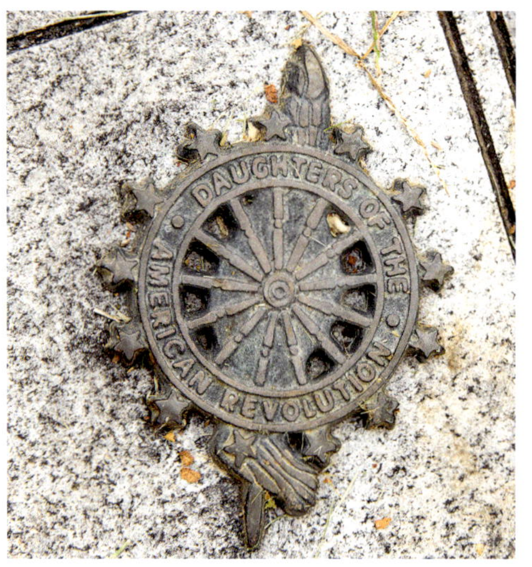

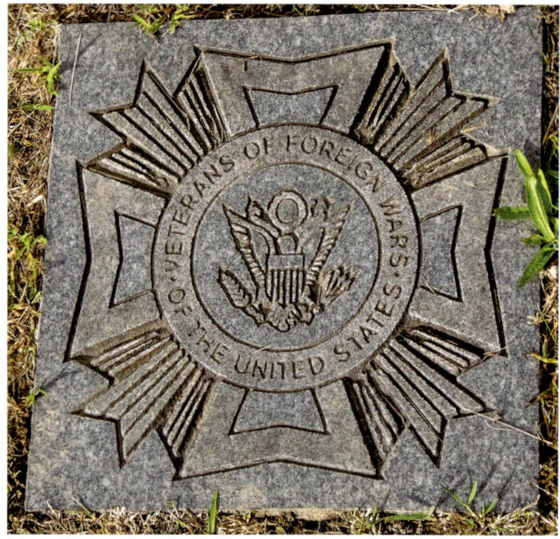

Above left: Daughters of the American Revolution Seal were established to keep alive the memory of those who fought in the Revolutionary War and tend the cemetery graves of their forefathers. The objective was to keep them in living memory as long as possible because they knew a nation that forgets would be in peril.

Above right: VFW plaque. Veterans of Foreign Wars is an organization that advocates for veterans and maintains veterans' graves in the U.S.

Below: Revolutionary plaque in Locust Grove Cemetery.

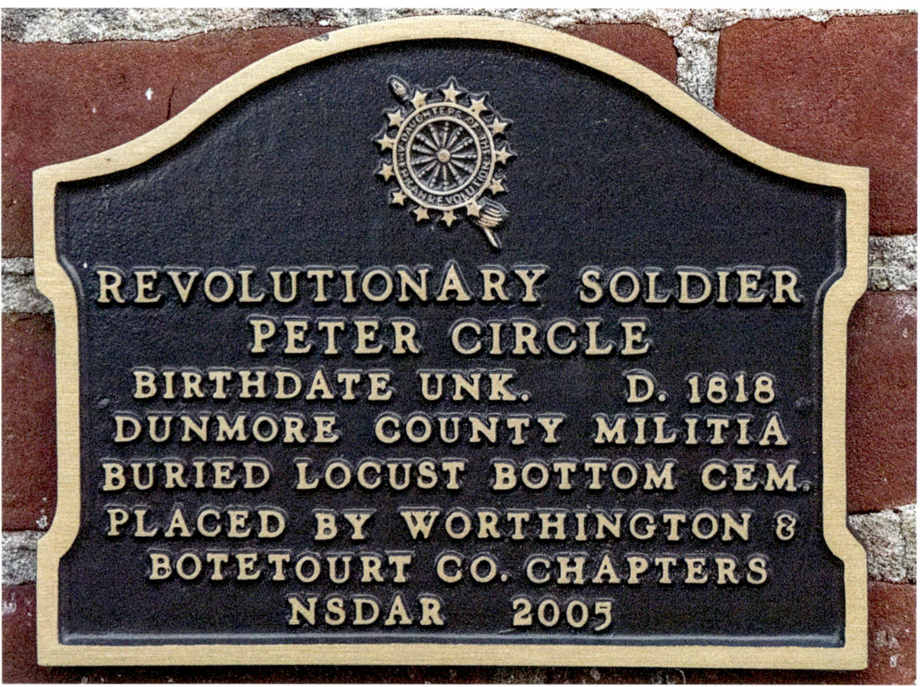

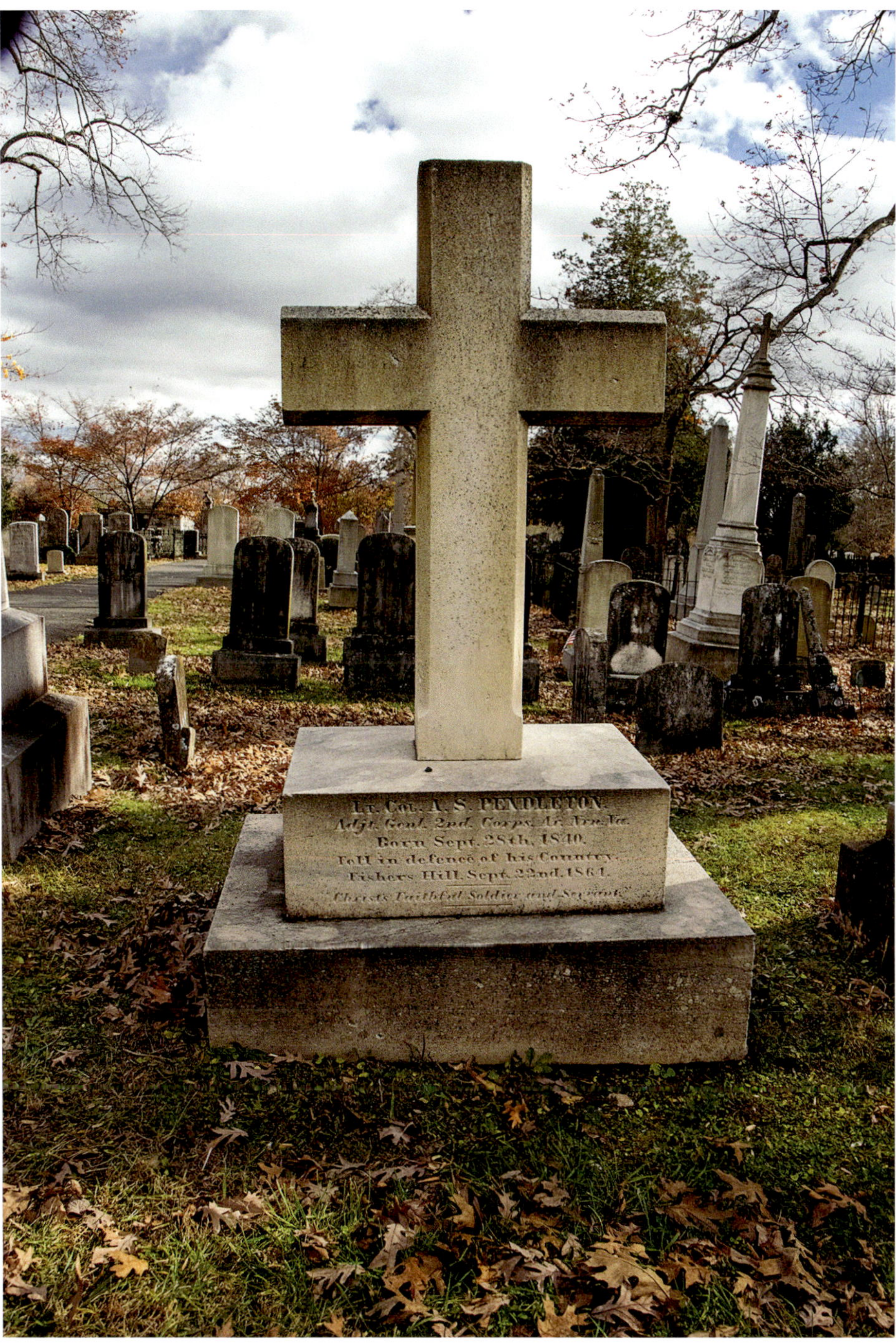

Lt. Col. Alexander Swift Pendleton. A confederate staff officer in the Army of Northern Virginia during the Civil War. Nicknamed Sandie, he served under Stonewall Jackson. He was wounded trying to rally men streaming to the rear and died the next day at Fishers Hill, September 22, 1864.

In Appalachia, these traditions held sway even after tradition and commercialism took hold, and funeral parlors and casket makers became commonplace. Even today in some very deep parts of the mountains these traditions are honored. And there is a movement taking place to move back to the old ways when it comes to end-of-life care of loved ones. These reasons range from economic to ecological. The commercialism that has pushed the expenses of burials to unmanageable levels is beginning to create serious pushbacks.

The tradition of adorning graves with flowers did not take hold until the mid-nineteenth century. These were not readily available or affordable for the typical Appalachian family. It was not uncommon, and is still frequently seen, to adorn graves with personal effects such as toys, pottery, shells, wreaths of wildflowers or vegetables, and, in later decades, crepe paper flowers. Pennies are also popular (a penny for your thoughts) to let the deceased know they are being remembered.

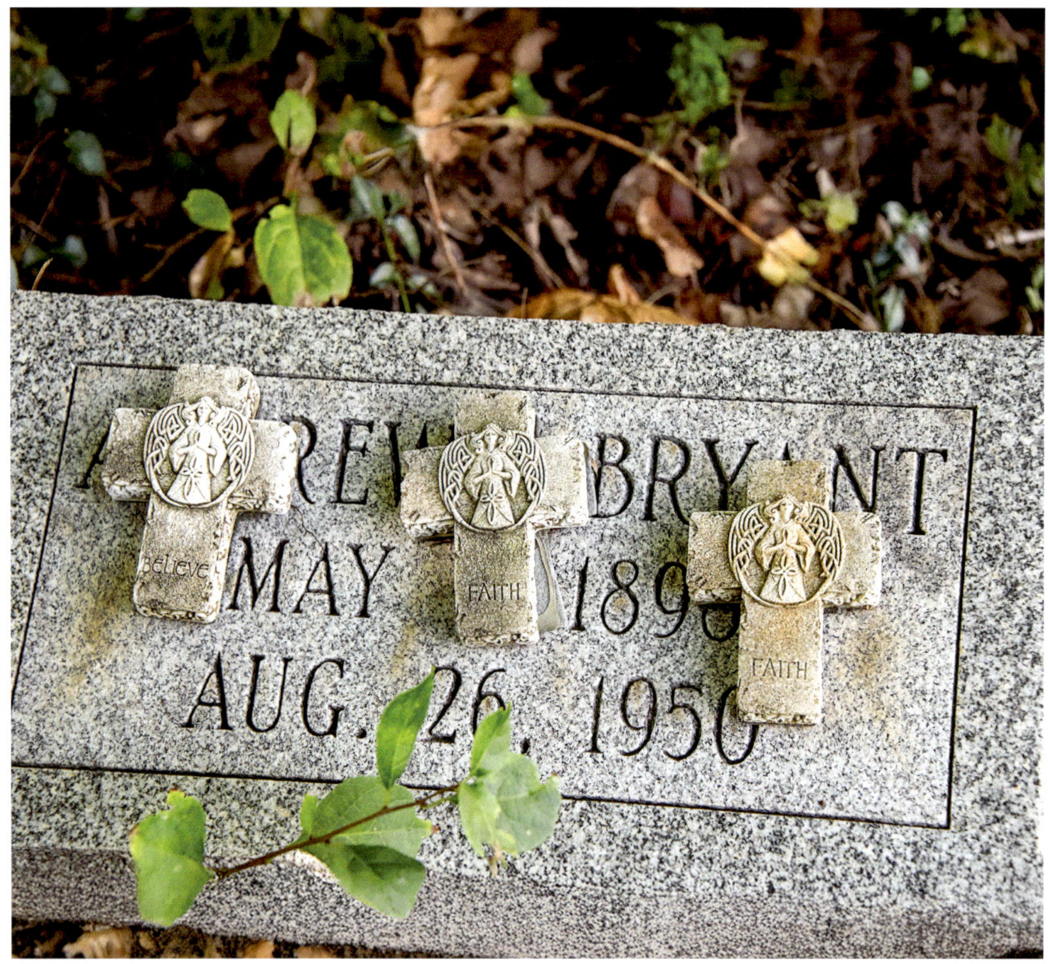

Small tokens left for a loved one are a common cultural norm in the region. Great thought is often put into the small items left to show loved ones they are remembered.

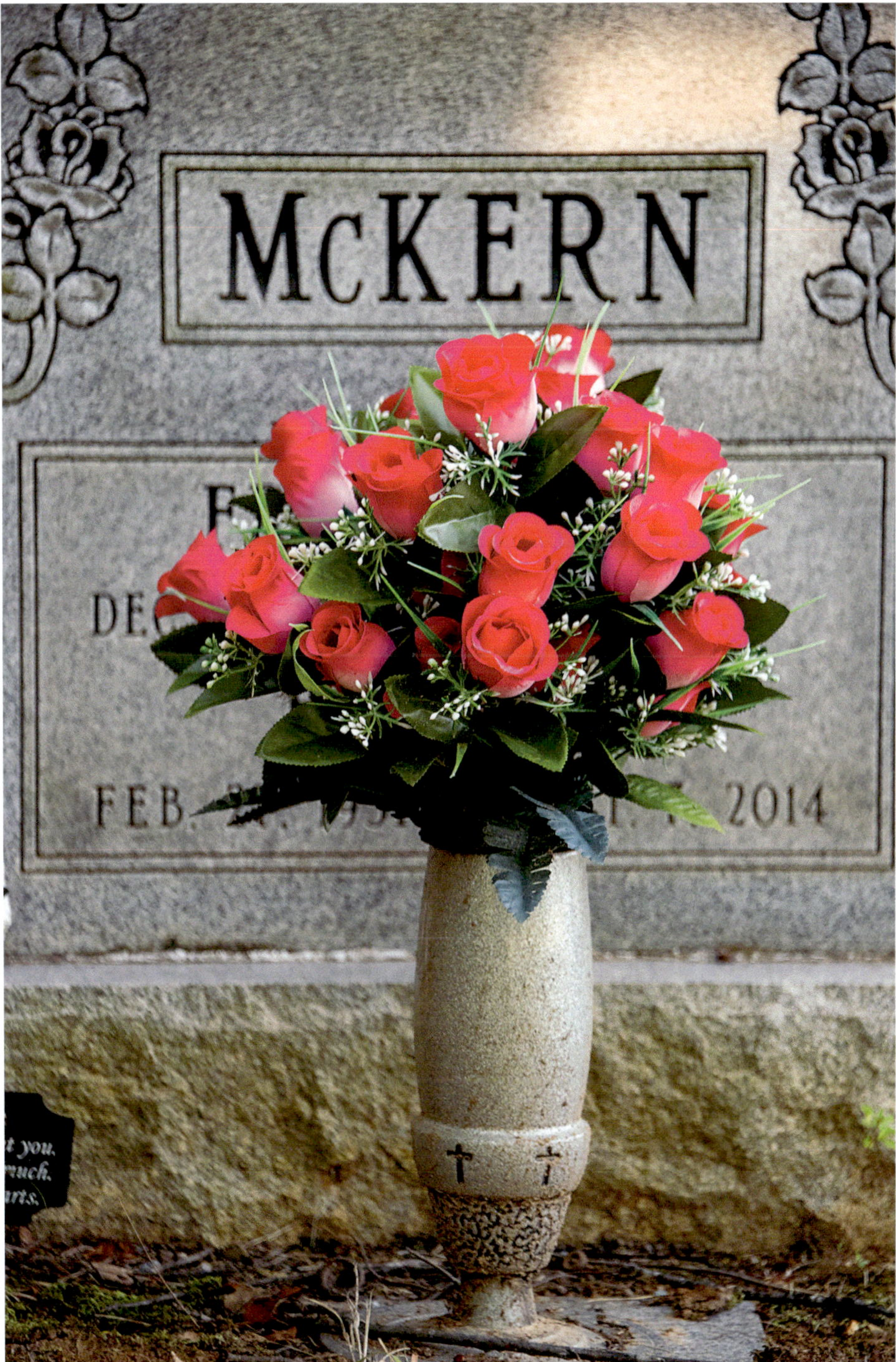

Flowers vases are often installed on a modern grave marker. For those more recently departed, it provides comfort for those left behind to visit and brings fresh arrangements whether real or silk.

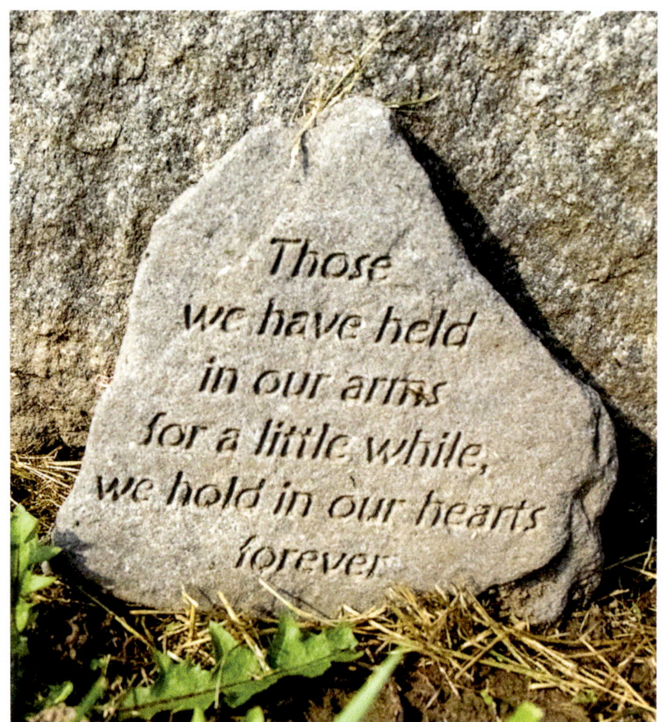

Many times, the small tokens on a loved one's grave bare a message to the loved one. "Those we have held in our arms for a little while, we hold in our hearts forever."

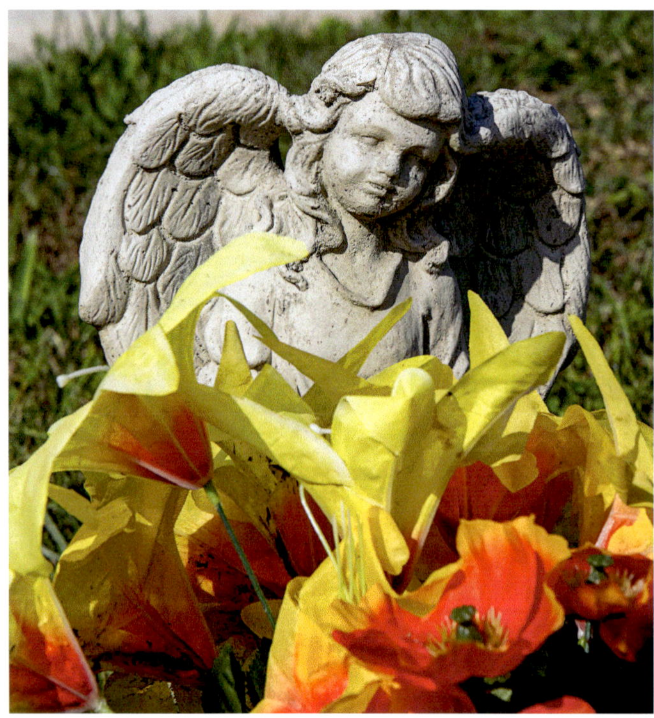

Flowers and tokens left on a grave give those left behind a way to express their feelings whether grief or just remembrance for loved ones.

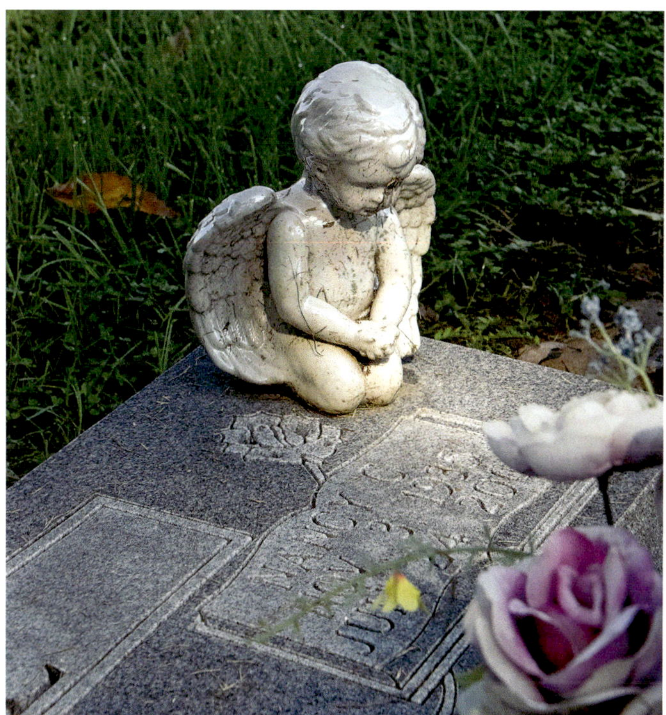

Angels are probably the most popular token left on a loved one's grave.

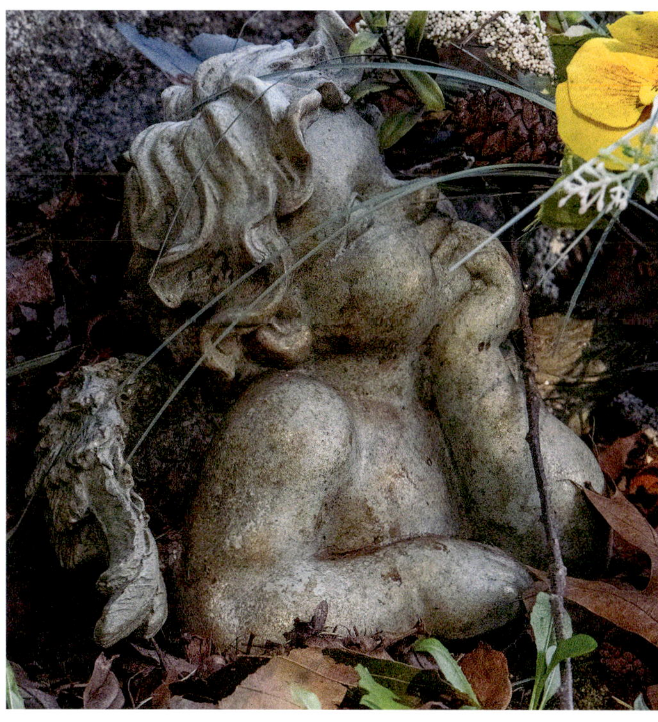

A small angel tucked in the flowers on a child's grave. A sort of hide and seek reflecting the sorrow for their passing.

In Appalachian culture, Decoration Day was a day in the spring when friends and relatives visited graves and brought memorial items to commemorate those who had passed. Many still do this in the spring once the weather turns nice.

There was a time in America, and in Appalachia, where it was commonplace to have a picnic by the graveside of your loved ones. During the nineteenth century, particularly in the later part of the century, graveyards and cemeteries were the closest thing to a park that existed. It is not uncommon today to find that older parks are adjacent to very old cemeteries, and this would be the reason why. It was also a way to include your deceased loved one in a family outing and show them they were not forgotten.

During this period, many of the deceased were young who died unexpectedly. Childbirth was often deadly; epidemics were common as were fatal accidents. Children were often the most vulnerable. Death was far more prevalent in the everyday. Coping with those deaths was a societal battle that affected communities. Before the age of grief groups and counseling sessions this also allowed people to come together with others who were facing the same struggles. It was an important social norm. Graveyards were also conveniently located next to church, allowing for Sunday picnics following services to visit loved ones and socialize with others who could understand. Cemeteries were also often central to the area churches, having the same advantages.

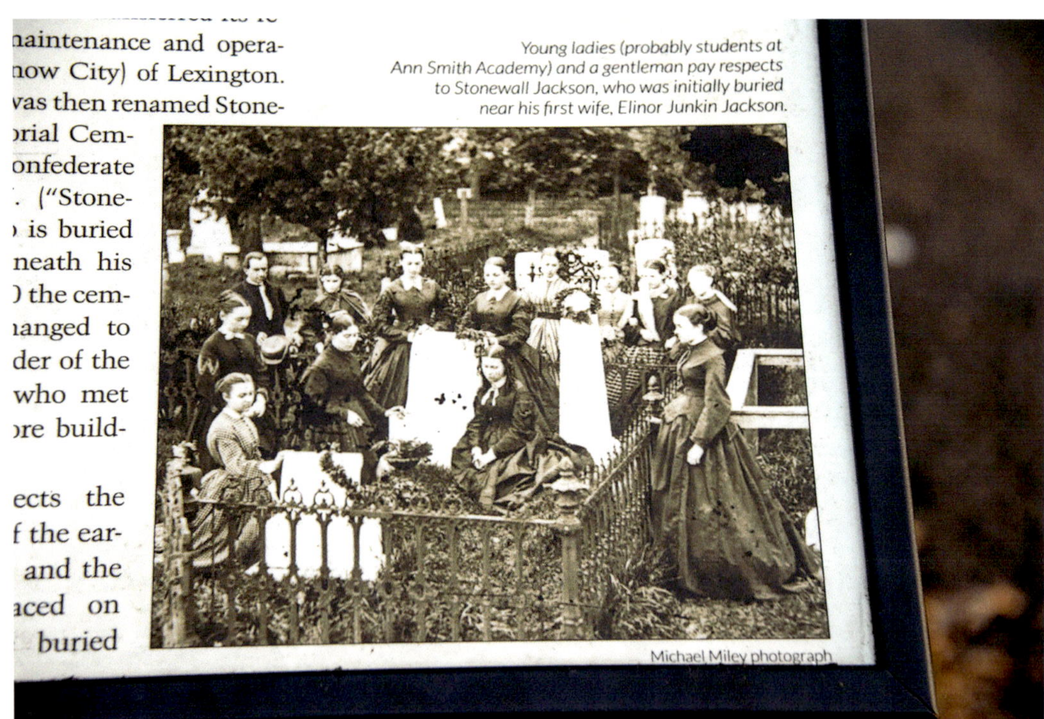

There was once a day every year in the spring when gathering in the cemetery was an annual tradition. It was known as Decoration Day and was an occasion for a family to gather to place flowers and tokens on a loved one's grave, tend the grave, and hold a memorial service. This tradition has long since been lost in most areas. A gathering in Oak Grove Cemetery, Lexington, Virginia.

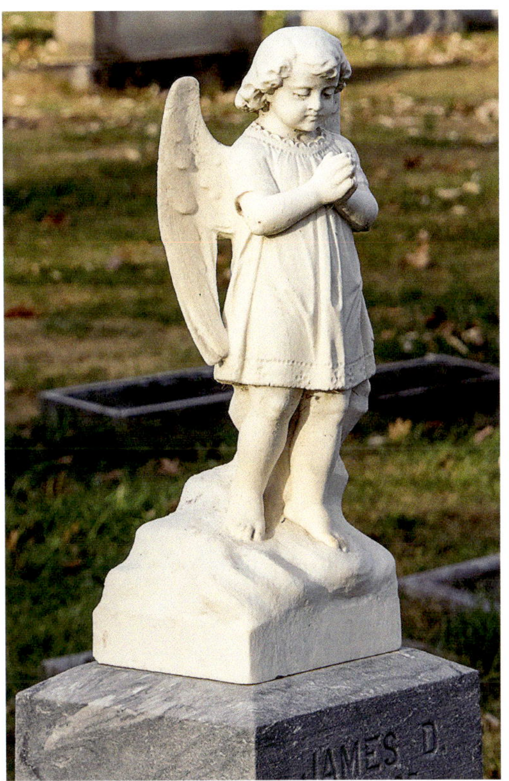

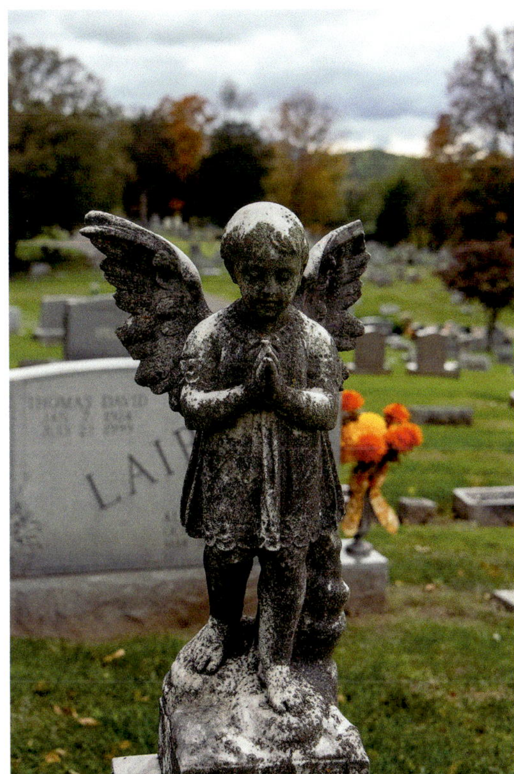

Above left: Angels are popular statuary and often added later. This one is in Oak Grove Cemetery in Lexington, Viginia.

Above right: Often evergreen trees are chosen for cemeteries because they are easier to care for and less to clean up after. However, they often leave behind discoloration on the stones. Weather and sun, combined with nearby trees and shrubs and the everyday dirt of the environment, cause the aged look, but also adds some degree of character.

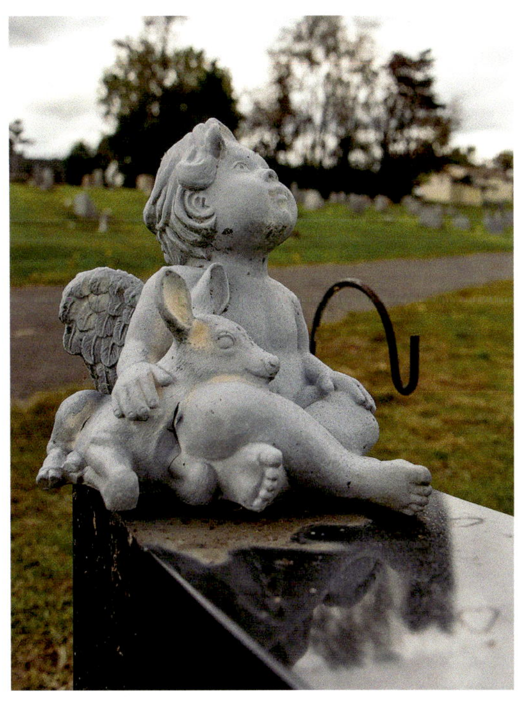

Right: A whimsical token left on a grave often gives comfort to the bereaved.

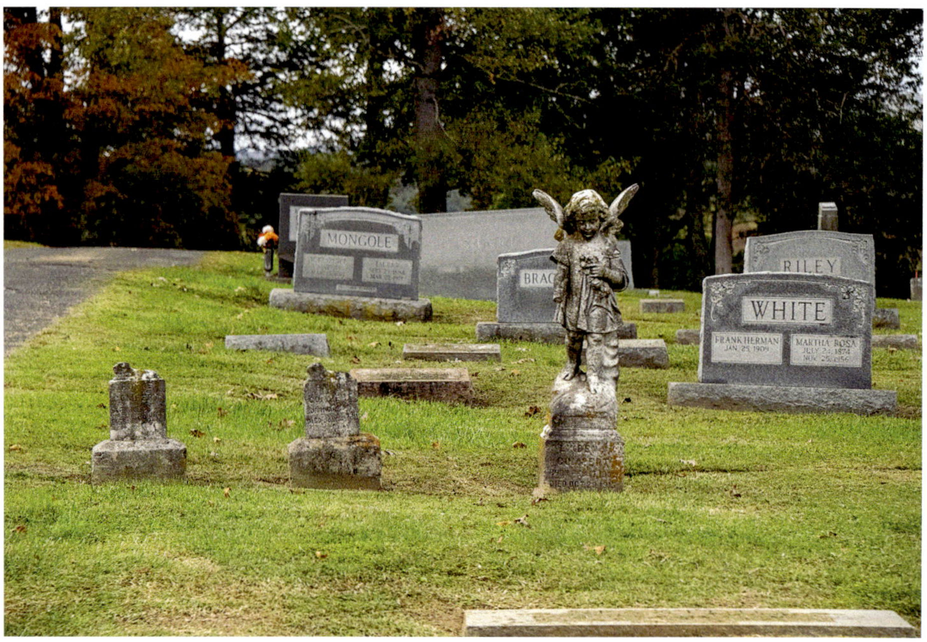

A line of children's graves in Cedar Hill Cemetery, Covington, Virginia.

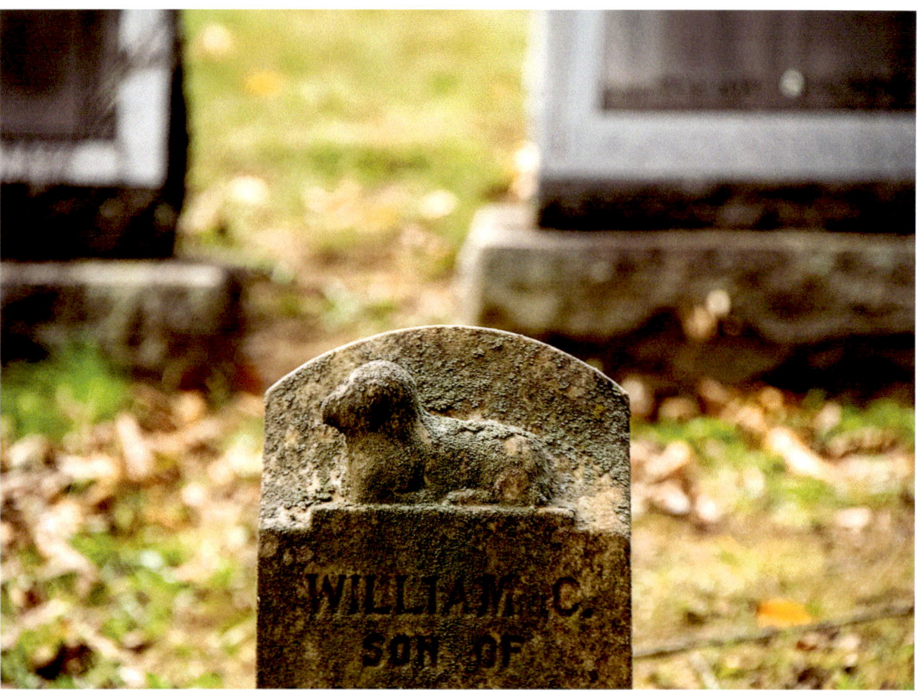

The lamb on child's tombstone has been a long-standing tradition on children's stones in the region.

Walk through any cemetery today and you realize they are a treasure trove of lost stories. Lives lived and lost. Triumphs and tragedy. Death mourned and life celebrated. There are symbols adorning stones that whisper secrets of the life lived by the occupant of that grave. From simple to elaborate each of them tell a story. The story may have fallen away over time as they were lost to the memories of the living, but that life was not unlike our own.

There is a common phrase that often appears on stones throughout the world, and Southwest Virginia is no exception. It was originally placed on the grave of Thomas Gooding in the seventeenth century. The original stone reads: "All you that do this place pass bye. Remember death for you must dye. As you are now even so was I. And as I am so you shall be. Thomas Gooding here do staye. Waiting for God's judgement daye." In today's cemeteries, it is more likely to be closer to the following: "Pause, stranger, when you pass me by: As you are now, so once was I. As I am now, so you will be. So, prepare for death and follow me."

Epithets, like symbols, vary widely for the stones that bare them. There are some short, many religious in bearing, a few are longer and still others tell an entire life's story. Keep in mind that the carvings were priced by the amount of carving to be done, which limited many to only the basics. The more carving, the more elaborate the stone, the more expensive it was likely to be.

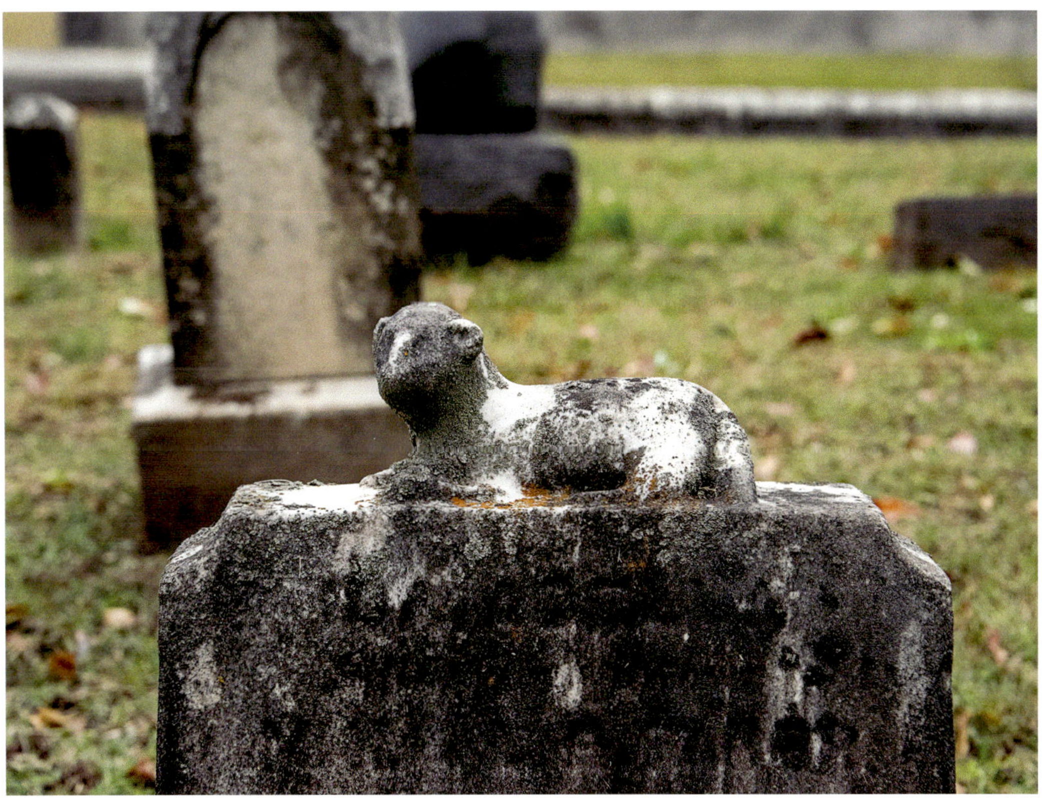

A lamb on a weathered tombstone of aged softer stone.

Markers in many of the small and quaint cemeteries were often homemade from the materials that were available. There was no money or time to retrieve carved foreign stone from many miles or even weeks away. The local stones were often limestone and other softer stones that would not wear well over time. Many are now only markers of unknown graves. Lost to living memory they go untended, their identities lost to time forever.

In both graveyards and cemeteries there are large open areas. These do have graves, but due to the limits of time and money many markers of the time they were buried were made of wood. Simple wooden crosses were common. In some cemeteries, non-descript stone crosses have been added to mark the graves. In others they are left unmarked and lost completely to time but for the acknowledgement that they are there.

Another aspect of unmarked graves has to do with slavery, segregation, and racism. Even in the mountains of Appalachia, one must remember that the populations of color were brought here mostly as slaves. This included African as well as native peoples indigenous to North America. There were also indentured servants who would never earn true freedom and were often referred to in later history as bond slaves. Of this group, there were few who truly cared for the dignity of these individuals' burials.

This book could not honestly depict cemeteries of this region, or any region in the U.S., without properly addressing this sad and sordid part of history. During the making of this book, a search for these cemeteries did not yield much information—for several reasons. It is a convoluted cultural legacy wherein there were a myriad of problems and "solutions" to this issue. The irrationality of the exclusion of burials based on racial divides and our own social identity and hierarchies to top it off are almost beyond comprehension today. We all love and care for our departed.

There are no identifiers on any stone encountered while writing this book that indicated a difference in race, only nationality and those of European nationalities. What is race, religion, or any other defining characteristic in the face of death, mourning, and burial? Still these instances of mortuary segregation, the political resistance they created, and the conflicts that arose creating segregation of even burial grounds are a haunting subtext to a dark part of history.

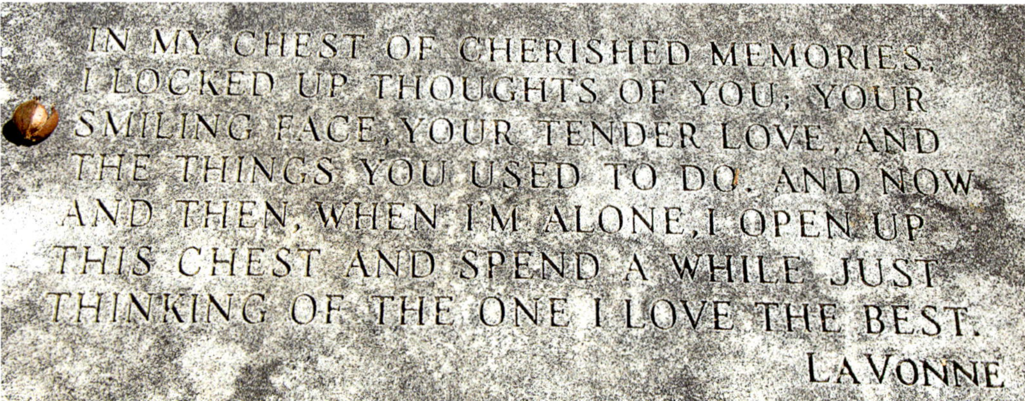

Epitaph to a loved one. The poem is more personal than the common inscriptions and this is not uncommon in this region. Often used are poems by favorite authors and even those written directly by the one grieving.

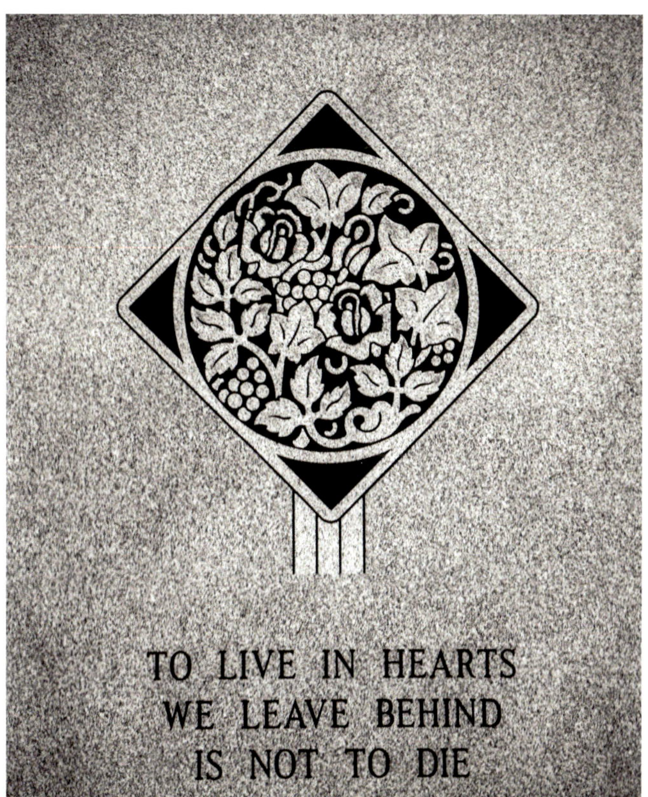

Right: Epitaph to a beloved family. "To live in hearts, we leave behind is not to die."

Below: Epitaphs to mothers seem to be the most common carvings in cemeteries throughout the region. A message to a beloved mother: "She was a tender mother here: and in her life the Lord did fear: We trust our loss will be her gain: And that with Christ she's gone to reign."

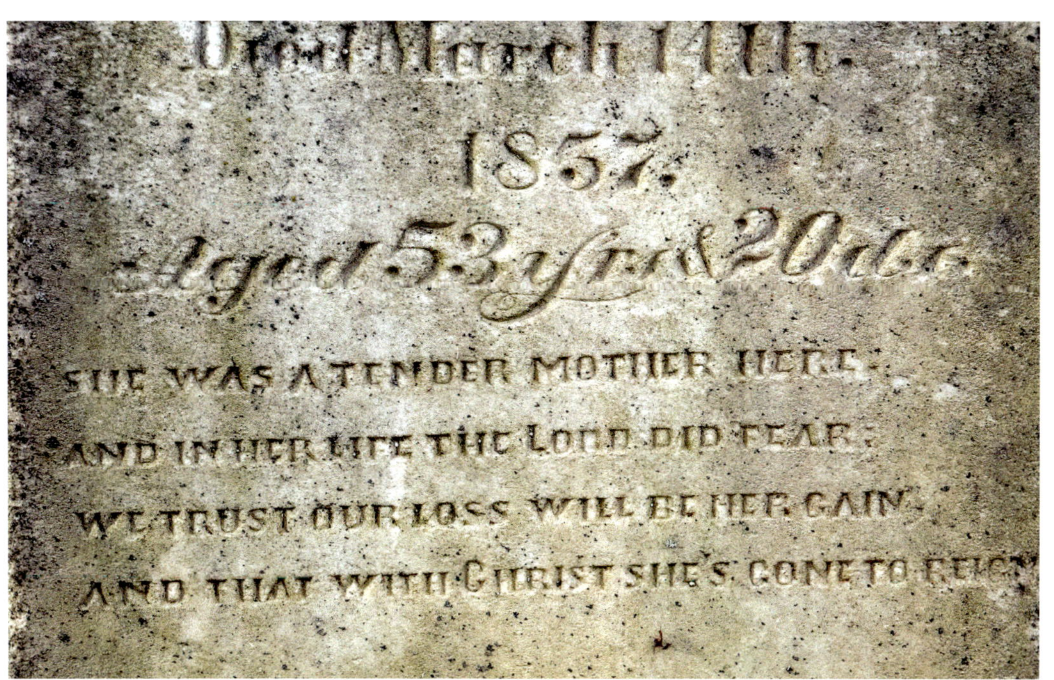

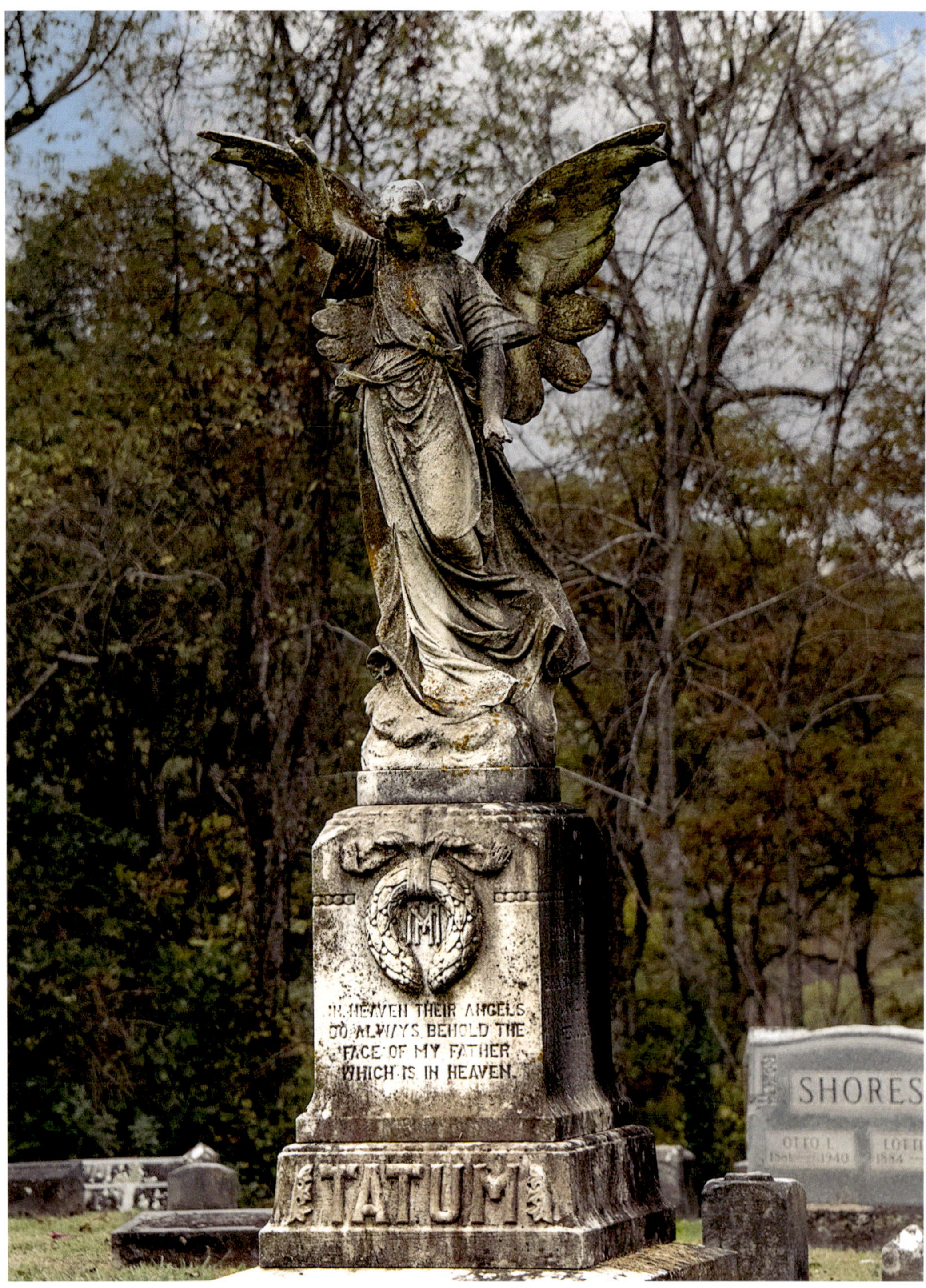

Also common are religious epitaphs like the one above: "In heaven their angels do always behold the face of my father which is in heaven."

Prior to the establishment of slave cemeteries and black cemeteries, it was common to discard non-white individuals in disrespectful ways. The graves were unmarked, in non-hallowed grounds. The ideal of privileged belonging in the U.S. unfolded across corpses, ashes, and burial grounds well into the mid- to late twentieth century.

The legal arguments that held this in place for so long were stated in a court ruling by Judge Joseph A. Mallery, Washington Supreme Court, in 1960:

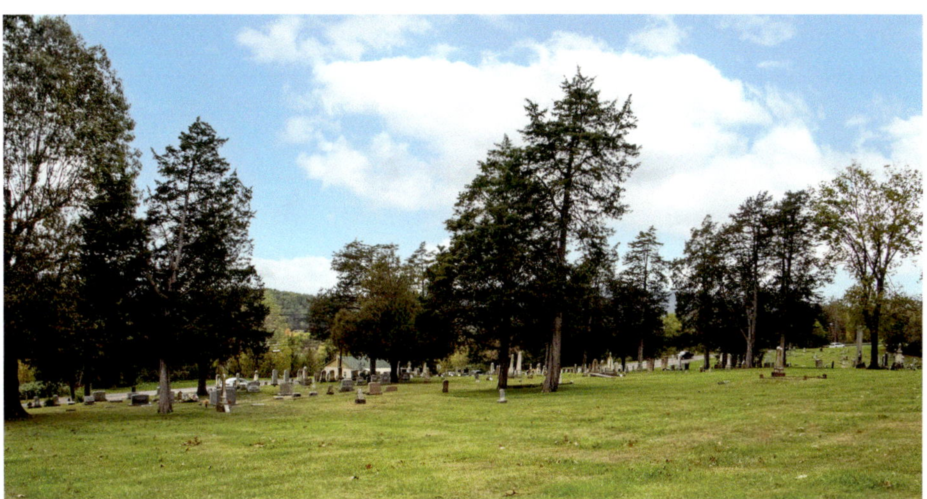

Cedar Hill Cemetery Slave Allotment is marked by cedar trees planted along its boundary, many of which have died, leaving a sparsely recognizable line. There was once a white picket fence also marking the boundaries, which no longer exists. Many of the markers would have been wooden and decayed long ago.

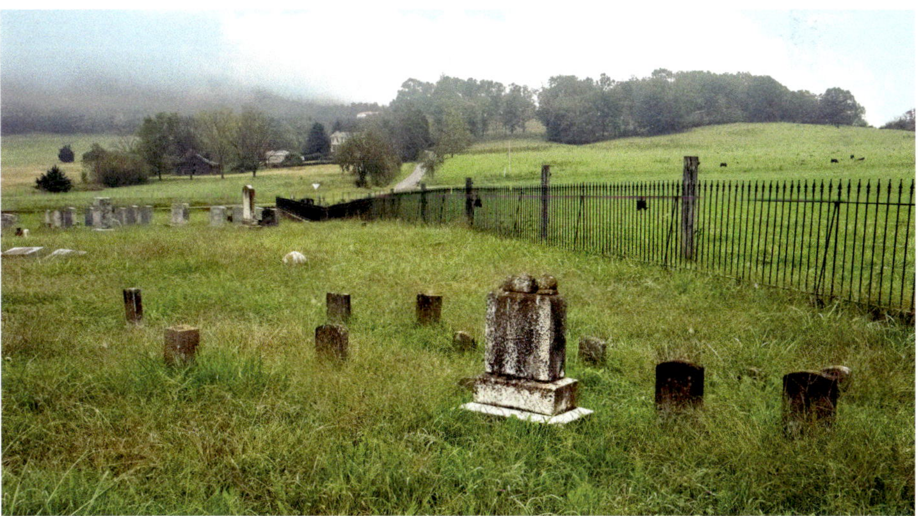

Worn and weathered stones and long stretches of wrought-iron fences mark the old cemeteries of Southwest Virginia as places of peace and grace. Locust Grove Cemetery.

> The undisputed facts in the instant litigation are that Evergreen Cemetery has segregated sections restricted to white children, Masons, veterans, Lutherans, and so forth. These restrictions implement the universal desires of religious, racial, and fraternal groups to be associated in death as well as in life. "Birds of a feather flock together."

The judge's ruling was invalidated the following year in 1961, when the state's legislature amended anti-discrimination laws to pertain to the disposition of human remains. Judge Mallery retired from the bench.

Other battles would take place which effect the rights to burial throughout the U.S. Chief Justice T. John Lesinski said it best when he stated: "When the law recognizes the philosophy represented by 'his own kind,' we are only a step away from adopting the racist philosophy which World War II was fought to eliminate."

If you would like to read more on this topic, please see the link to the article "Grave Matters: Segregation and Racism in the U.S. Cemeteries" in the caption. The Order of the Good Death has done an excellent job of approaching this topic.

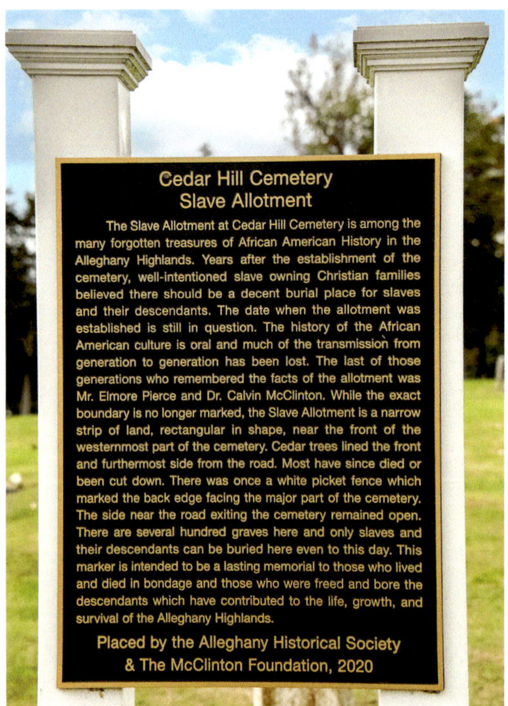

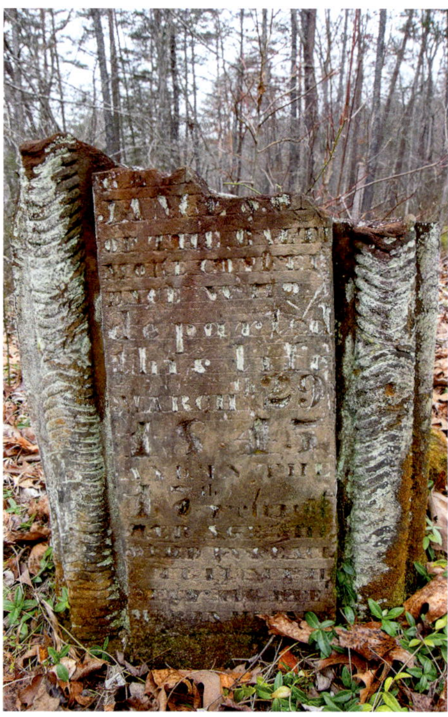

Above left: A dark shadow in the history of the region was the treatment of slaves in regard to cemeteries. Eventually well-intentioned families sought a decent burial place. That was when the Cedar Hill Cemetery Slave Allotment came about. For a long time, its history was lost. It is now marked, and burials of decedents are still allowed. The above historic marker was placed by the Alleghany Historic Society and McClinton Foundation.

Above right: German-style carving in McCartney Cemetery, Craig County, Virginia, damaged due to vandalism.

In many of the cemeteries stand incredible old trees. After a visit to a few of the older cemeteries, it becomes apparent that trees are as much a part of the landscape as are the stones themselves. The trees have unique folklore of their own, which made their way into the spirituality and superstition of cemeteries. It was not uncommon for trees to be planted in the place of headstones or placed with a small stone to mark a burial in the early days of Appalachia. The availability of stone or the manpower it took to carve a stone was somewhat limited. Wooden markers were not uncommon and would degrade over time, leaving only the tree to stand in testament.

In Southwest Virginia cemeteries oak trees are particularly prevalent. The folklore of the oak is found throughout history from the Celts to the Greeks. It's at the heart of ancient beliefs and traditions, many of which came here with European settlers. Oaks were planted in most of Appalachia's cemeteries for not only its folklore, but as markers. Oaks were planted to stand watch as guardians over the boundaries of cemeteries and graveyards. Even though there were not necessarily religious reasons in the case of graveyards, which were primarily built with the religion of that church, it was a throwback to the blending of pagan and Christian traditions. They were revered for their strength, longevity, and considered protectors. The size of the full-grown trees made them stand out, denoting the boundaries and perhaps adding some degree of intimidation.

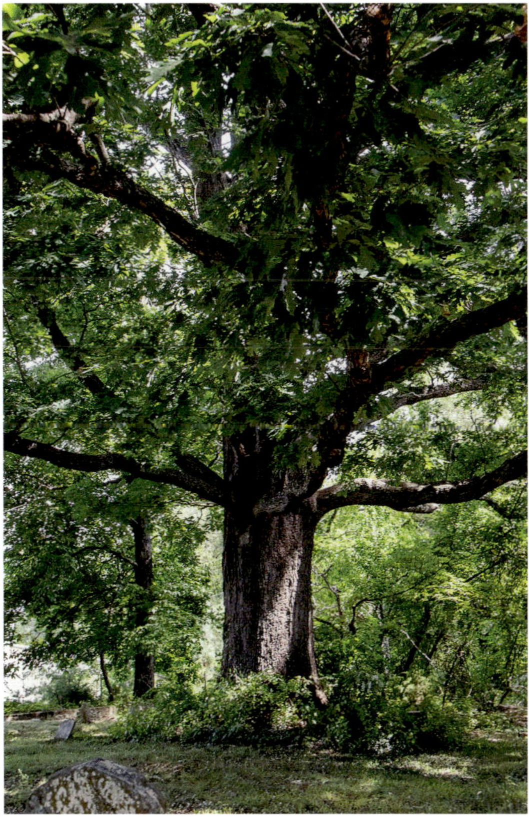

Tombstone Cemetery still hosts one of the oldest oak trees in the region. It stands beside the Denton Monument and marks the boundary of the cemetery.

Elm trees were very popular substitutes for oak trees on cemetery boundaries, but due to diseases specific to elms, many are no longer in existence. Oak trees are also facing similar challenges, and it is not uncommon to see only the remains of a stump where these gentle giants once stood.

Yew trees are probably one of the most well-known in most areas because of their ability to thrive in nearly any condition. It is one reason they are so long-lived. They have a long history that goes back through Christian storytelling to pagan roots. They were sacred to a list of deities and goddesses and were said to purify the dead and were used in death rituals.

In more modern beliefs, they represent rebirth and resurrection. The representation of eternal life is somewhat ironic, as the tree contains taxine, which is an alkaloid poison. This was a solid reason to keep livestock out of graveyards as well as deterring wildlife, thus helping preserve the grounds. In superstition, they also deterred ghosts, thus discouraging the soul from lingering.

Cedar trees are very common in the older cemeteries of Southwest Virginia. The evergreen is thought to symbolize eternal life since it does not shed for the winter. To the Cherokee, the cedar wood held the spirits of their ancestors. It is also a common belief that burning cedar during ceremonies carries prayers to heaven. Cedar is often used to drive out negative energy and purify land, homes, and anything else that needs cleansing.

Another less-known use in the case of Southwest Virginia was as a dividing line at the edge of cemeteries denoting the common burial ground and the slave burials once plots were finally established.

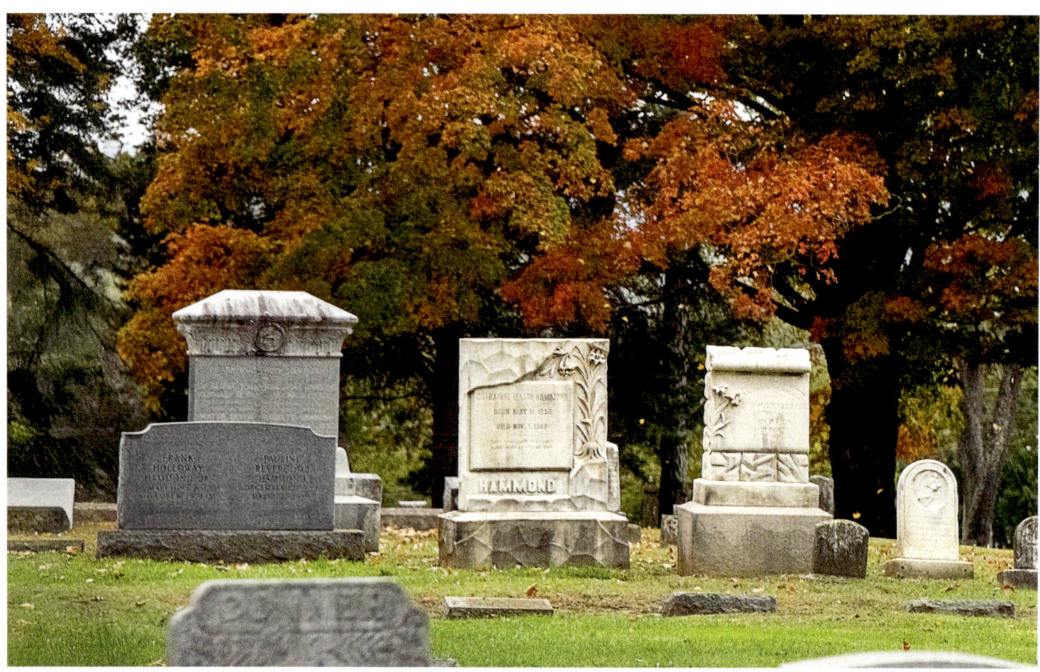

The oak trees in Cedar Hill Cemetery stand along the old boundary before the cemetery was expanded. The white and grey stones stand out against the fall colors.

Cypress trees are also known for their ability to grow just about anywhere and their resilience. There seems to be some disagreement as whether the tree represents death or eternal life. Celts placed their dead in the tree for burial and it was sacred to the underworld. In more recent times, they are chosen for their aesthetic as "mournful trees." They seem to express sorrow because they are dark and gloomy. They are a warning that one is entering a place of death.

The most unique stone in Southwest Virginia was not for anyone of historic note or wealth. It was for a much-beloved little boy who had captured the hearts of everyone who loved him, including the carver Lawerence Krone. Krone was a close friend of the family who had taken him in when he was deathly ill. He carved the stone for free in gratitude for their kindness.

It stands in the Old Tombstone Cemetery in Roanoke, Virginia, and is a monument for nine-year-old Robert Denton. It is a monolithic freestone carving by Lawrence Krone. Mr. Krone is known for his folk-art tombstones found throughout Southwest Virginia, but this is the most notable of his creations and is the only signed work.

It is listed on the national Register of Historic Places and Virginia landmarks Register. Robert Denton died in 1805. His tombstone is a caving of a sarcophagus with the top portion exposed. It once held a stone lid depicting the child; however, grave robbers stole that portion. As a result of intentional vandalism and the very special nature of his tombstone, the historic site has been fenced off to protect it.

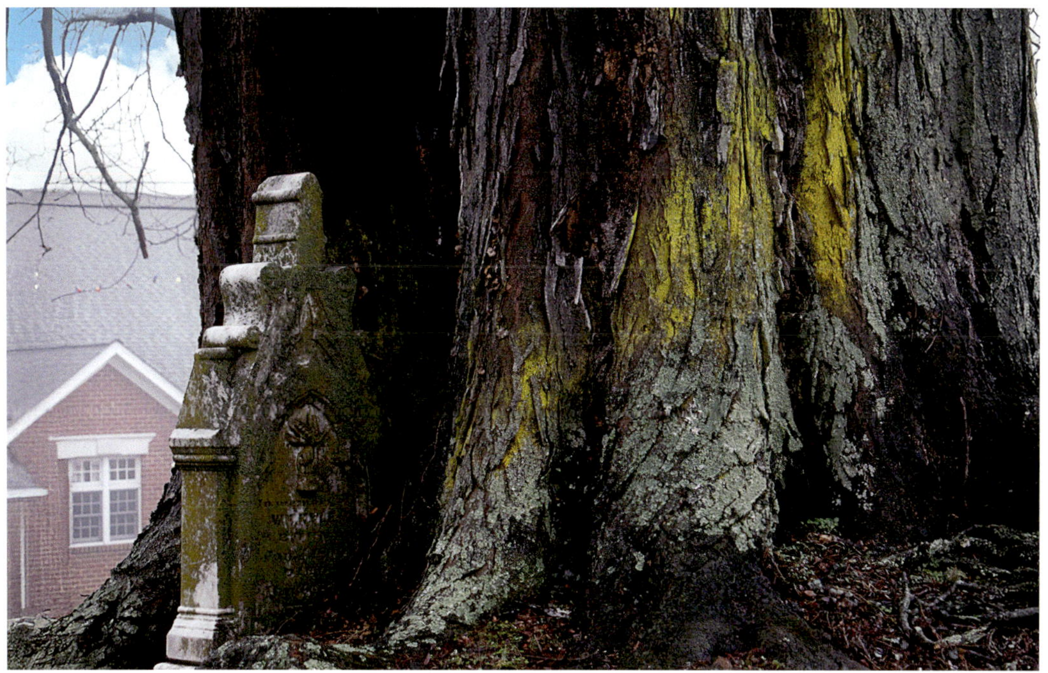

An ancient honey locust tree in Godwin Cemetery, Fincastle, Virginia. The tree has grown to embrace one of the oldest cemetery stones. The tree is so large and old it is on the National Registry. Its age is approximately 210 years old, but its size is second largest in the nation. Honey Locust are native to Virginia.

Lawrence Krone was a prolific Virginia-German carver. He was a lifelong member of the German Reformed Church and well known for his folk-art tombstones. They tend to be more personal and ornate, featuring hand-carved designs, epitaphs that tell a story about the deceased and intricate symbols. Krone's German-style tombstones are characterized by not only their intricacy, but by double sided designs and motifs.

Lawrence Krone was a notable influence on the cemeteries of Southwest Virginia during the early 1800s not only for his beautiful and unique stones, but also for his influence on other monuments. This influence is felt in many of the old cemeteries as an attempt to emulate his mastery. Many of those carvers, unfortunately, did not use materials that will last for centuries and are already showing the wear of weather and time.

The carving design he used for the Denton Monument was commonplace in New England during the period, however, it is unique to Southwest Virginia. Even more unique is that the stone is carved in three languages: German, Latin, and English. In part, the inscription reads: "Once loved, once valued, now avails me not; Though my relations have not me forgot..."

Two other works of Krone's stand in Southwest Virginia. The McGavock Family Cemetery, which is a private family cemetery on private property and not covered in this publication due to privacy issues and vandalism concerns.

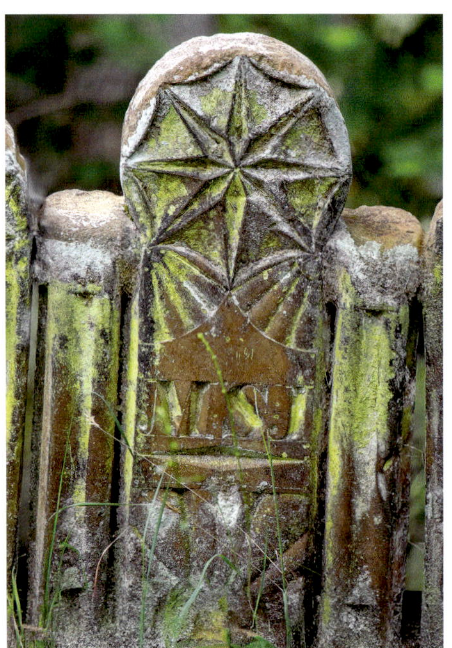

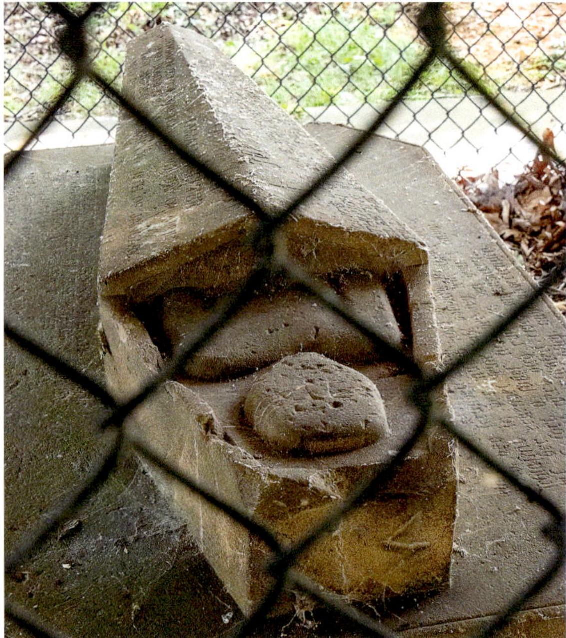

Above left: German carver style (carver unknown), initials of decedent only, in McCartney Cemetery, in the woods of Craig County, Virginia.

Above right: The Denton Stone was carved for nine-year-old Robert Denton in the form of a sarcophagus. It was a common design in New England during the era, but unheard of in the Southwest Virginia region. Today, it is missing the cover that would have portrayed the occupant.

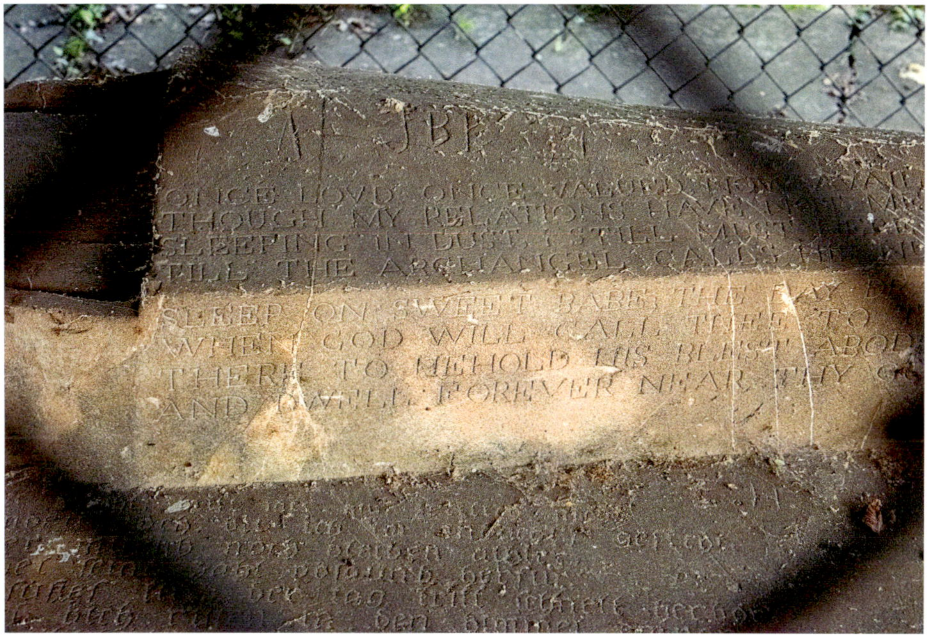

The Denton Stone was carved in three languages: English, German, and Latin. The carver was a dedicated friend of the family who carved the memorial to the young boy.

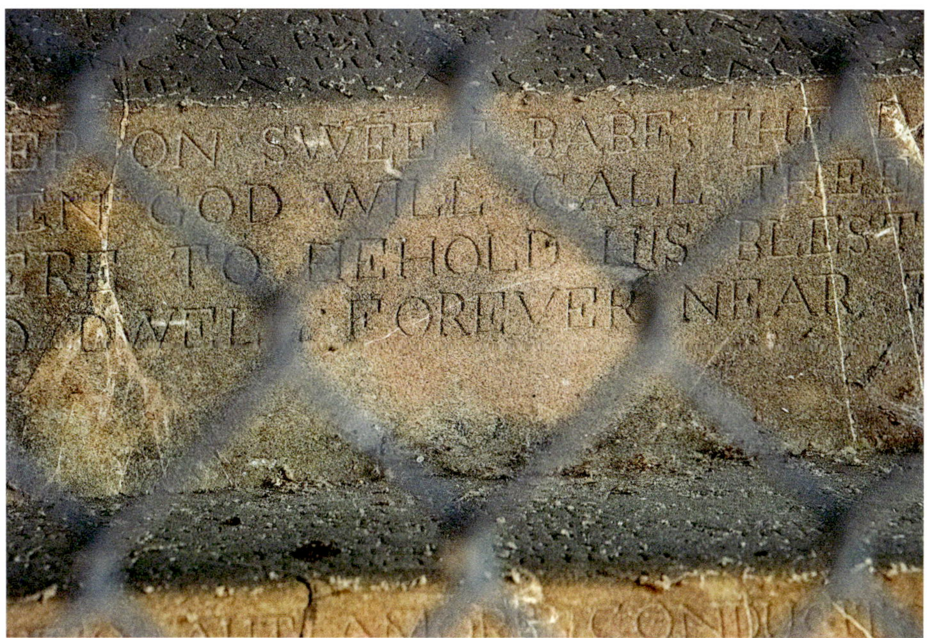

Denton Monument: folk art tombstone carved by Lawrence Denton around 1805 for nine-year-old Robert Denton. "Once Loved, one valued, now avails me not; Though my relations have not me forgot..."

The other is in the graveyard of St John's Lutheran Church and Cemetery, located in Wythe County. This cemetery contains around thirty early nineteenth-century German-style stones. The one most notable, carved by Krone, is for the Minister George Daniel Flohr, 1826.

After the Industrial Revolution took hold, large cemeteries were more common. There was money to erect more impressive monuments of varying materials. Clifton Forge Virginia holds one of these cemeteries.

Built into the steep hillside above the town is the Crown Hill Cemetery. Many of the internments here show the opulence of an age that Appalachia had not previously known. The Alleghany region in which it is located is central to the City of Covington—which was and still is known for lumber, and Iron Gate (once notable for iron)—and is the Western Gateway to Virginia through the Allegheny Mountains. This created an area that produced an influx of wealth reflected in the monuments of its cemeteries.

Clifton Forge was originally a land grant in 1770 to Robert Gallaspy by Lord Botetourt, who was at the time the governor of Virginia. The settlement developed along both sides of the river. The town developed into an important railroad hub during the industrial revolution and grew with industry. It was a major maintenance facility for steam locomotives for the Chesapeake & Ohio Railroad and was a boomtown employing nearly 2,000 people just with the railroad.

The hub was conveniently central to multiple industries creating an opportunity for a particularly interesting cemetery to emerge. Today it stands on the hill overlooking the town and the mountains that gave rise to those industries. After the near total collapse of the industries that fed it C&O Railroad was eventually absorbed into other companies and the hub was closed, ending the railroad industry that employed most of the town.

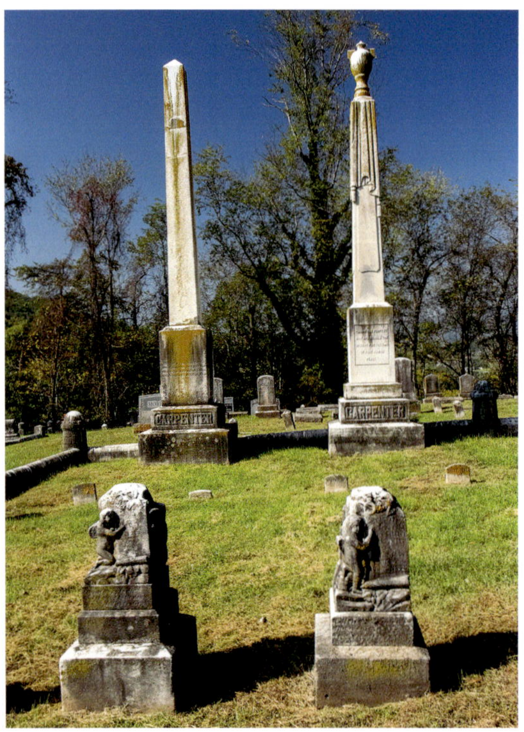

The grandeur of the Industrial Revolution shows up in the cemeteries of the towns it enriched. The period was one of wealth and this was reflected in opulence even for the dead.

Not far from Clifton Forge is one of the most notable cemeteries in Southwest Virginia: Lexington's Oak Grove Cemetery. It was originally the Presbyterian Cemetery but was renamed in 1949 after the confederate general buried there, Stonewall Jackson Memorial Cemetery. It was established in the late 1700s by the church and is now owned by the city. There are over 140 veterans of the Revolutionary and Civil Wars, Margaret Junkin Preston (the Poet Laureate of the Confederacy), and two governors of Virginia: John Letcher who died in 1864 and James McDowell who died in 1846. It was renamed in 2020 following the protests throughout the U.S. and the movement to remove confederate names from publicly owned locations as well as the abundant statuary. The statuary over notable graves was not disturbed.

Oak Grove's location near Virginia Military Institute (VMI) is not by chance. It's a reflection of its proximity to many influential people who were founders of not only the country but of VMI and Washington & Lee University. There are two Virginia governors, four generals, a founder of VMI, and members of the Virginia Convention that would ratify the U.S. Constitution. There are also innumerable other officers and citizens who were founders in various stages of the United States.

Modern cemeteries are losing the personalization, grace, and grandeur of those of earlier centuries. For decades, the movement has been underway to close the old cemeteries to further additions as their plots are filled. This pushes burials into new, more convenient memorial gardens where there are no stones above ground level, but plaques flat to the ground, mausoleums and columns for depositing cremation urns. Along with forbidding stones came the installation of monuments to honor not individuals, but the dead in general. This is shifting in many of these burial grounds to non-descript religious symbolism, mostly of Christian faith.

Alongside these changes there is a movement towards more natural burial grounds. Green burial is a trend toward places where one can be laid to rest in a more natural setting. Eco-friendly alternatives to traditional cemeteries. While there is interest, there is currently only one natural burial alternative in Southwest Virginia, adjacent to an existing traditional cemetery. Forest Rest Natural Cemetery located in Boones Mill, Virginia. In the interim, there are efforts to make the burial grounds more natural by means of returning to the tradition of including trees extensively to the landscapes rather than monuments that do not represent the permanent residents of the memorial gardens.

Everything from ornamental trees to the more traditional oaks, elms, and evergreens are being added to the landscape plans of the modern cemeteries, bringing them full circle. For the time being, it is a bridge between modern cemeteries and green burials, creating aesthetically pleasing grounds that are closer to parks than barren fields.

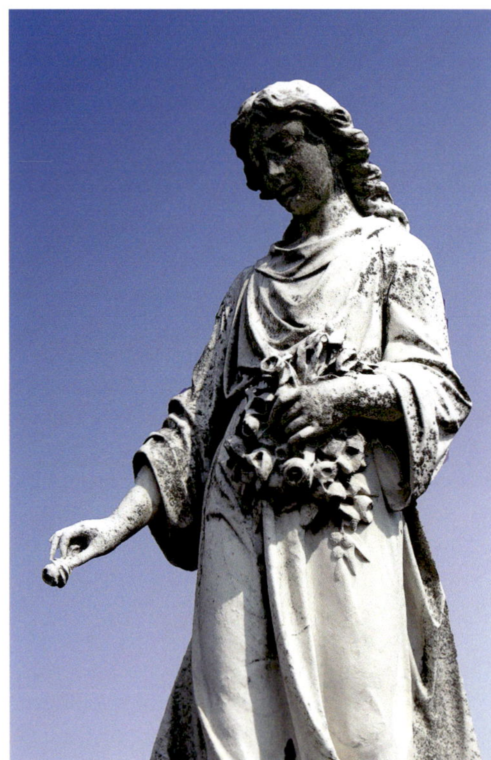

Left: Religious statuary representing entire sections of cemeteries is now the only above ground stones allowed in newer cemeteries. Inground markers make mowing and maintaining modern cemeteries easier. Fairview Cemetery, Salem, Virginia.

Below: Modern cemeteries are starting to return to earlier designs. Shrubbery and a memorial park theme closer to the older Garden Cemeteries.

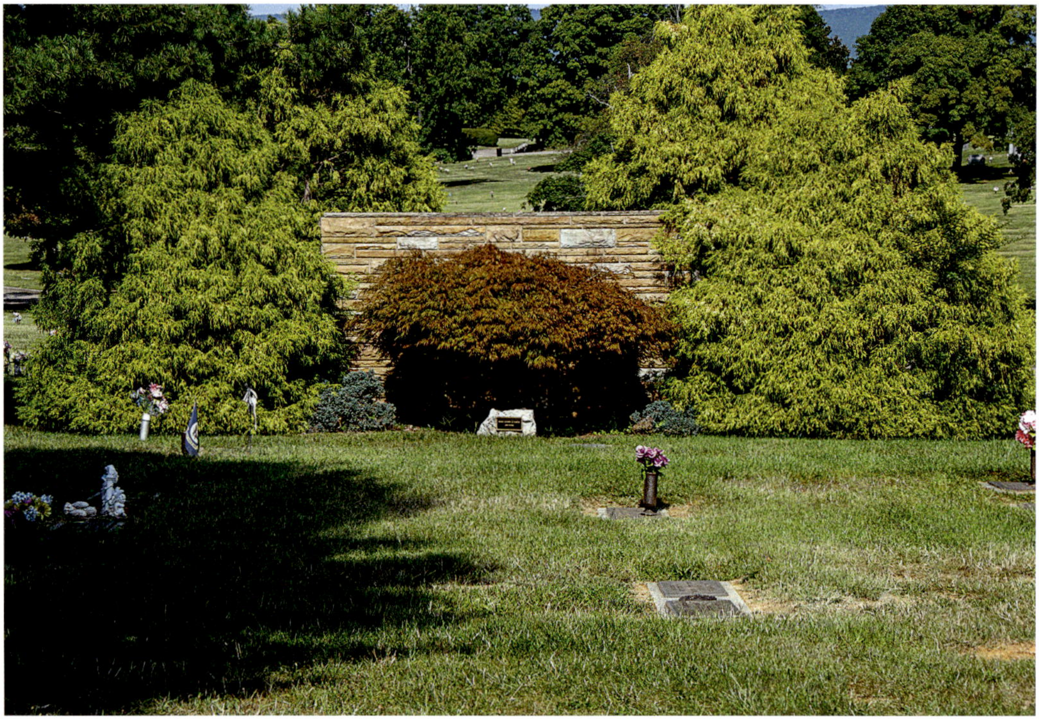

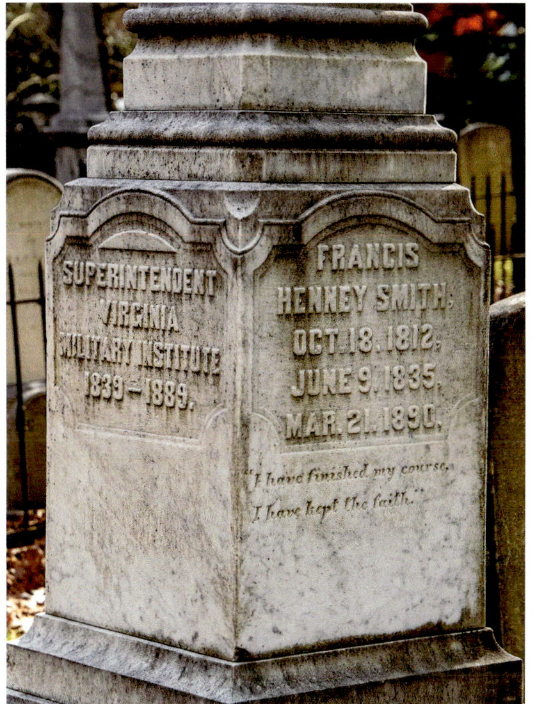

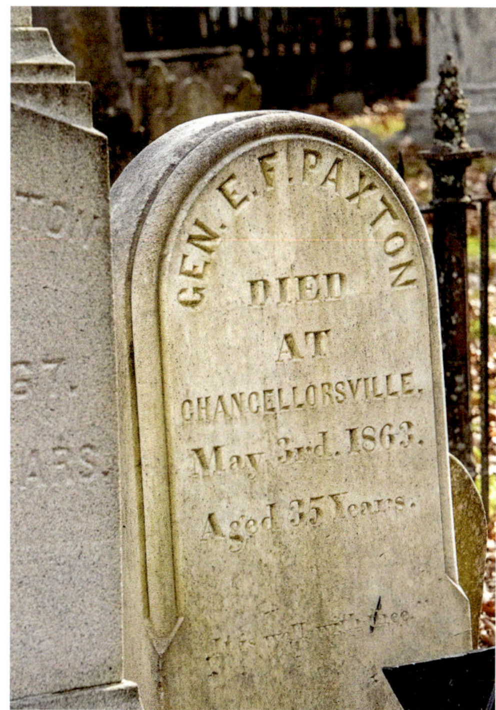

Above left: Francis Henney Smith was the Virginia Military Institute's first superintendent. He graduated from the United States Military Academy and serviced as a second lieutenant in the U.S. Army before becoming a professor of mathematics at Hampden-Sydney College until he was recruited to the opening of VMI.

Above right: Elisha Franklin Paxton was a lawyer and soldier serving in the Confederate Army during the American Civil War. He fought at the 1st Battle of Bull Run and was elected a Major of the 27th Virginia Regiment in 1861. In 1862, he was promoted to brigadier general and led the Stonewall Brigade at Fredericksburg and Chancellorsville where he was killed in battle in May 1863.

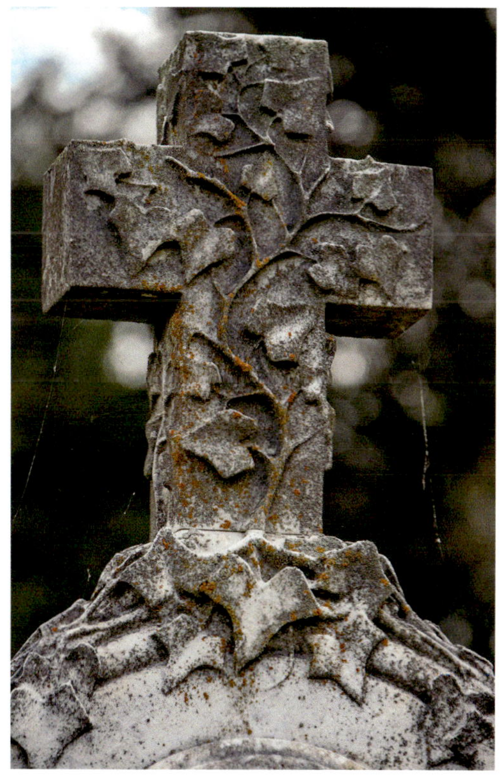

Right: Cross embraced in vines, representing immortality, friendship, and everlasting life, in Covington's Cedar Grove Cemetery

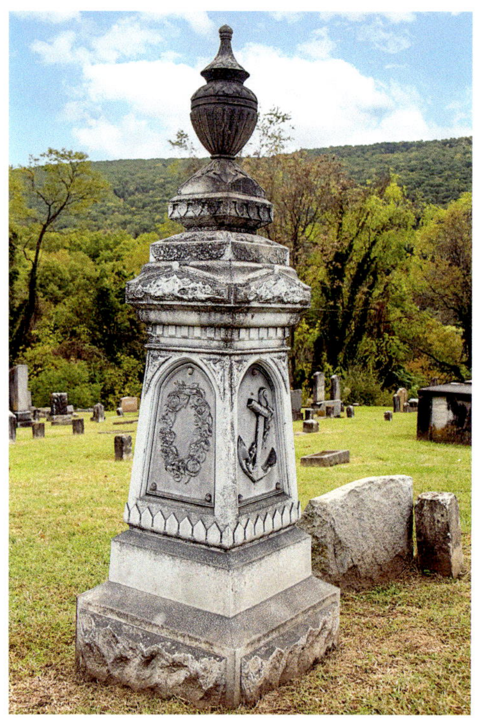

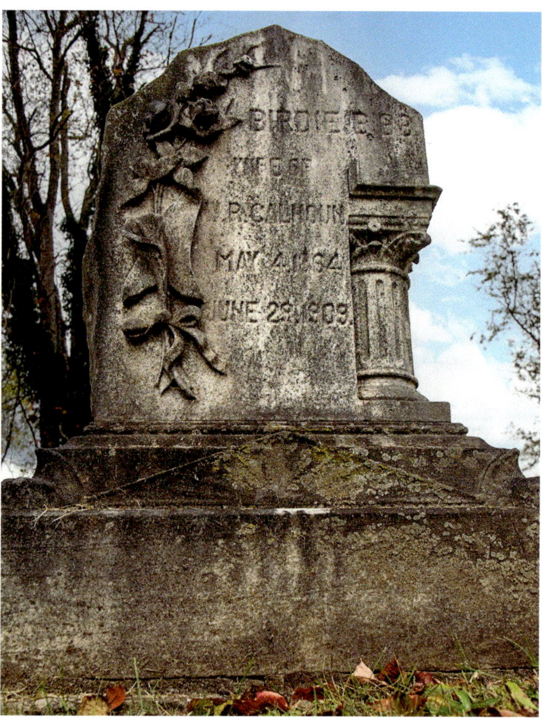

Above left: This stone looks different because it is made of iron. Most likely it represented the industry in which he made his fortune. The symbols on the grave marker, the anchor could have been the assurance of life after death, or he may have been a mariner. The wreath represented victory, distinction, and eternal life and often represented someone who excelled.

Above right: Stone carvings during the boom period of Clifton Forge spared no expense as seen in the elaborate nature of this stone. The flower representing a life lived, the stone column showing classical strength and stability. The Calli lily represents her marriage and fidelity.

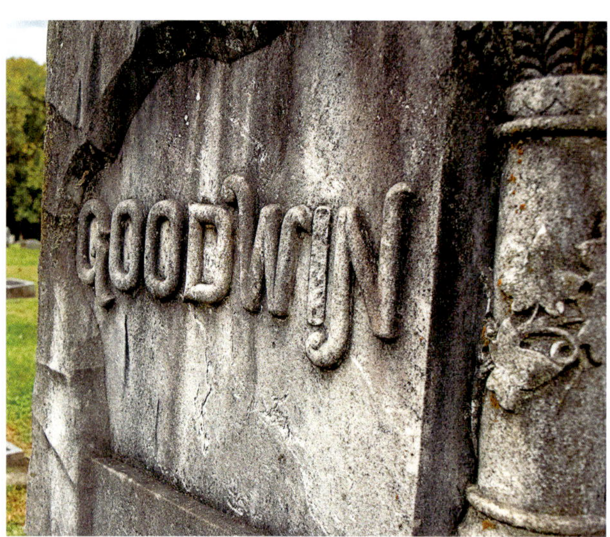

Left: Family monuments denoting importance were carved of great slabs of granite, which was an expensive stone for the time.